Westchester County

A Pictorial History

second printing 1989

Westchester County
Historical Society

2199 SAW MILL RIVER ROAD
ELMSFORD, NEW YORK 10523
(914) 592-4323

Three-legged Race at Rye Beach
Courtesy of Westchester County Historical
Society

Westchester County
A Pictorial History

**By Susan Cochran Swanson
and Elizabeth Green Fuller**

Design by Jamie Backus Raynor
Donning Company/Publisher
Norfolk/Virginia Beach

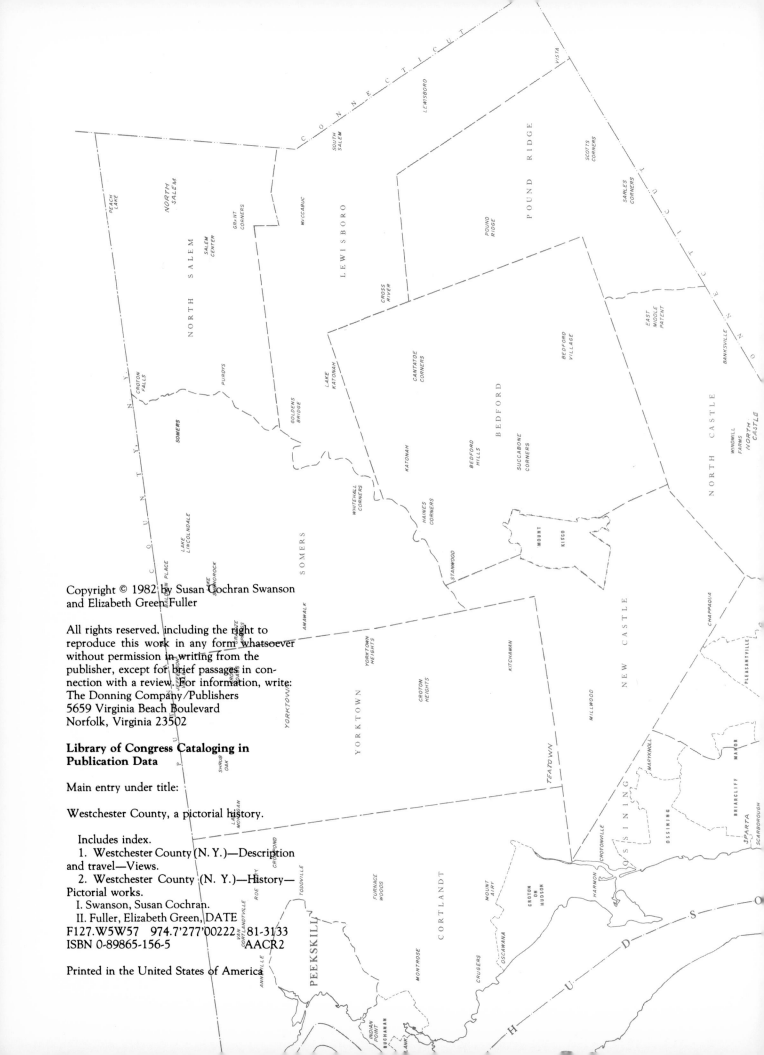

**Library of Congress Cataloging in
Publication Data**

Main entry under title:

Westchester County, a pictorial history.

   Includes index.
   1. Westchester County (N. Y.)—Description
and travel—Views.
   2. Westchester County (N. Y.)—History—
Pictorial works.
   I. Swanson, Susan Cochran.
   II. Fuller, Elizabeth Green, DATE
F127.W5W57   974.7′277′00222   81-3133
ISBN 0-89865-156-5   AACR2

Printed in the United States of America

Contents

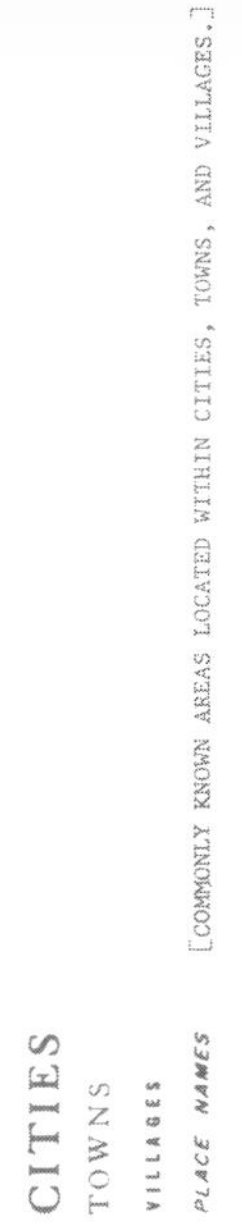

CITIES
TOWNS
VILLAGES
PLACE NAMES
[COMMONLY KNOWN AREAS LOCATED WITHIN CITIES, TOWNS, AND VILLAGES.]

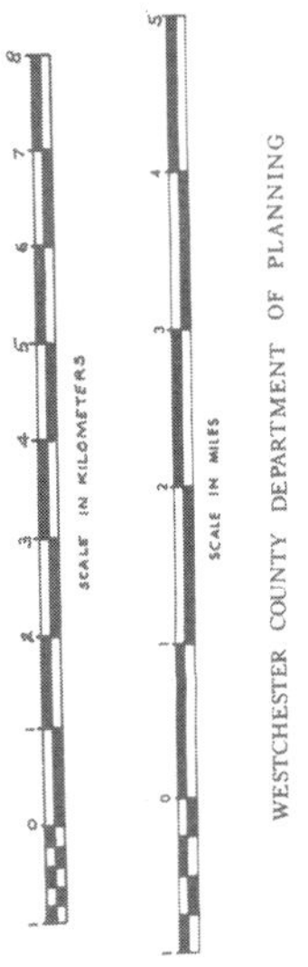

SCALE IN KILOMETERS
SCALE IN MILES
WESTCHESTER COUNTY DEPARTMENT OF PLANNING

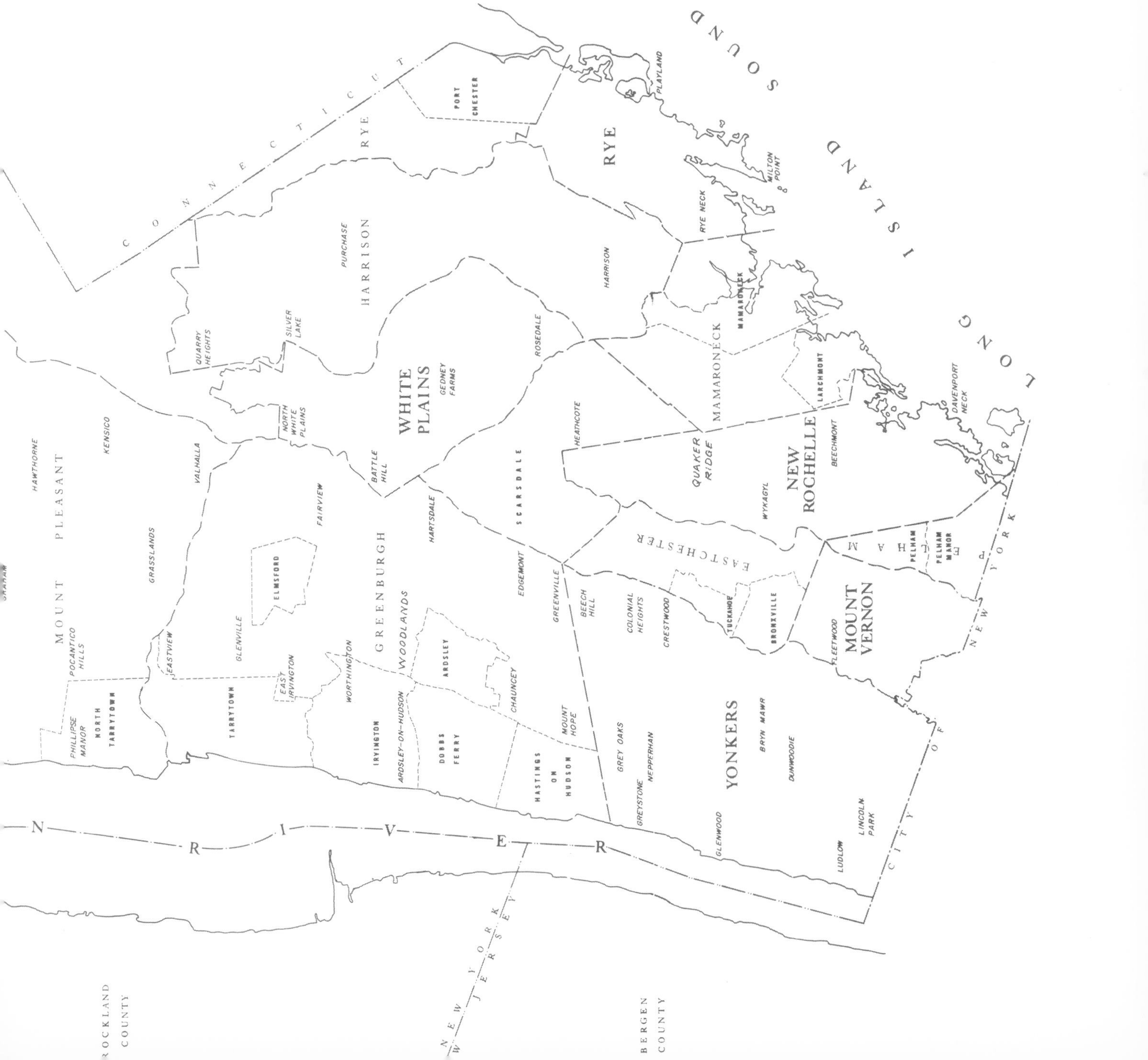

CONNECTICUT
LONG ISLAND SOUND
PORT CHESTER
PLAYLAND
RYE
MILTON POINT
RYE NECK
HARRISON
PURCHASE
MAMARONECK
LARCHMONT
DAVENPORT NECK
WHITE PLAINS
GEDNEY FARMS
ROSEDALE
SILVER LAKE
QUARRY HEIGHTS
NORTH WHITE PLAINS
BATTLE HILL
HEATHCOTE
QUAKER RIDGE
NEW ROCHELLE
BEECHMONT
WYKAGYL
SCARSDALE
HARTSDALE
EASTCHESTER
PELHAM
PELHAM MANOR
MOUNT VERNON
TUCKAHOE
BRONXVILLE
CRESTWOOD
COLONIAL HEIGHTS
BEECH HILL
GREENVILLE
EDGEMONT
MOUNT PLEASANT
HAWTHORNE
KENSICO
VALHALLA
FAIRVIEW
GRASSLANDS
ELMSFORD
GREENBURGH
WOODLANDS
ARDSLEY
CHAUNCEY
POCANTICO HILLS
GLENVILLE
EASTVIEW
EAST IRVINGTON
WORTHINGTON
TARRYTOWN
NORTH TARRYTOWN
PHILLIPSE MANOR
IRVINGTON
ARDSLEY-ON-HUDSON
DOBBS FERRY
HASTINGS ON HUDSON
MOUNT HOPE
GREY OAKS
GREYSTONE
NEPPERHAN
YONKERS
BRYN MAWR
DUNWOODIE
GLENWOOD
LUDLOW
LINCOLN PARK
LEETWOOD
CITY OF NEW YORK
RIVER
NEW YORK
NEW JERSEY
ROCKLAND COUNTY
BERGEN COUNTY

Dear Friends:

For those of us who call Westchester our home, there is a tremendous sense of pride in the knowledge that our county is about to celebrate its Tricentennial. There is also a special sense of wonder in the realization that the past 300 years have produced a historic richness and cultural diversity which are unmatched by many other locations.

I am indeed pleased to introduce this pictorial history of Westchester and to invite you to trace our growth and development through its unique and impressive series of photographs. I am also delighted to congratulate this volume's co-authors for their success in creating a living legacy to our county's past and present greatness.

—Alfred B. DelBello
County Executive

Foreword

The authors of pictorial histories frequently begin their work from the base of a collection of photographs, prints, and other graphic material which they deem worthy of publication and then attempt to make their books "history" through chronological arrangement and descriptive words. The results may be interesting but not necessarily histories.

Elizabeth Fuller and Susan Swanson have not fallen into this trap. As true professionals in the historical field and lively writers as well, they began with an outline of the 300 years of Westchester history, and they culled from the wealth of material available to them the very best graphics to illustrate the period and matched this material with highly literate copy to create a historical record. The result is a treat for the eye and the intellect.

Westchester could not have grown to its present stature without the dedication and dreams of imaginative and effective citizens. The authors recognize this fact, and their book has many personal stories and reminiscences of those who have contributed so much to the county.

Westchester County: A Pictorial History is more than a social history of a county. It is an engaging, well-written and documented record of three centuries of growth in an area which has always provided leadership for America, both in men and ideas.

—Richard Maass
Westchester County Historian

Preface and Acknowledgements

Westchester County: A Pictorial History could not have been written without the generous co-operation and support of many people throughout the county. We felt from the beginning that in order for the book to be a true representation of 300 years of Westchester's history, we had to go directly to the county's more than forty-five communities. We visited every town in Westchester and spoke with town historians, librarians, and members of local historical societies. In each town and village we found dedicated people eager to share their time and knowledge, as well as photographs collected over the years illustrating the history of their area.

Westchester is composed of four distinct geographical areas. White Plains, the county seat, divides largely rural northern Westchester from the more populous southern region, and the hill towns on the Hudson River contrast sharply with the shore-front communities along Long Island Sound. Rather than to present a pictorial history of each separate community or region, our objective has been to integrate pictures from each area into the 300-year history of Westchester as a whole. We collected more than 600 photographs. Making the final selection of 350 pictures to tell this history was an extremely difficult task. We thank all those who allowed us to use their photographs, as well as the talented experts who aided in the many phases of the book's production.

In particular we would like to thank Gray Williams, Jr., of Chappaqua, whose artistic, photographic, and editorial expertise was invaluable. Richard Lederer, Jr., Scarsdale Historian, gave countless hours of advice, assistance, and moral support. Richard Maass, County Historian, read the text for historical accuracy and generously loaned his priceless manuscripts for inclusion in the book.

The following people and organizations from each Westchester community provided photographs, information, and guidance: *Bedford:* Donald Marshall, Bedford Historian; Lloyd Cox, Jr., and Phyllis Dix of the Bedford Historical Society; Lino Lipinsky of the John Jay Homestead, Katonah; Katonah Village Library; and Caramoor, Katonah. *Cortlandt:* Jane Northshield, Croton-on-Hudson Historian; Anne Marie Burke, Buchanan Historian; Croton-on-Hudson Public Library; Julianna Free-Hand of Croton; and Consolidated Edison Co. of New York, Inc. *Eastchester:* Jean Bartlett, Bronxville Historican; Harriet Bianchi and Madeline Schaeffer of the Eastchester Historical Society; Bronxville Public Library; and Doris Bouton Tether of Bronxville.

Greenburgh: William Emerick, Ardsley Historian; Barbara Novich of the Ardsley Historical Society; Tema Harnick of the Dobbs Ferry Historical Society; Ann Blatt of the Greenburgh Public Library; Lee Schmidt of the Elmsford Historical Society; Karolyn Wrightson and Virginia Maguire of the Hastings-on-Hudson Historical Society; Hastings-on-Hudson Public Library; Florence Levines of the Jasper Francis Cropsey Museum, Hastings-on-Hudson; St. Andrew's Golf Club, Hastings-on-Hudson; Adele Warnock of the Irvington Historical Society; Helen Lynch of the Irvington Town Hall Theatre, Inc.; Julius LaRosa of Irvington; Daniel Girard, Tarrytown Historian; Adelaide Smith and Marie Peters of the Historical Society of the Tarrytowns; Union Carbide Corporation, Tarrytown; E. W. Axe and Co., Tarrytown; Cathy Steves and Nancy Gold of Sleepy Hollow Restorations, Tarrytown; and Richard Slavin of Lyndhurst, Tarrytown. *Harrison:* Rosemary O'Connor and Edythe Caro of the Charles Dawson History Center; and S.U.N.Y. Purchase. *Lewisboro:* Alvin Jordan, Lewisboro Historian; Colleen Dewhurst of South Salem; and Nicholas Shoumatoff of the Delaware Indian Resource Center, Trailside Museum, Ward Pound Ridge Reservation, Cross River.

Mamaroneck: Burton Meighan, Mamaroneck Historian; Grace Pugh of the Mamaroneck Historical Society; Judith Spikes, Larchmont Historian; Sydney Astle of the Larchmont Historical Society; and the Larchmont Public Library. *Mount Kisco:* Kenneth Morgan, Mount Kisco Historian; Ira Finke of the Mount Kisco Historical Committee; Dr. and Mrs. Robert Patterson; Kathy Berger; and the *Patent Trader. Mount Pleasant:* Edmund Cox, Mount Pleasant Historian; John Crandall, Pleasantville Historian; Carsten Johnson of the Pleasantville

Historical Society; Barbara Seibert of Pleasantville; Claire Collier of the Rockefeller Archive Center, Pocantico Hills; and Patricia Higgins of the Reader's Digest Association, Inc., Pleasantville.

Mount Vernon: Virginia Moskowitz, Mount Vernon Historian. *New Castle:* Frances Cook Lee, New Castle Historian; Evelyn Arcuni of the Chappaqua Historical Society; and Ruth Ann Kniffen of Chappaqua. *New Rochelle:* Thomas Hoctor, New Rochelle Historian; Florence Stapleton and Mary Alice Richardson of the Huguenot-Thomas Paine Historical Association; and the College of New Rochelle. *North Castle:* Richard Lander, North Castle Historian; Lindsay H. Welling, Jr., and Doris Watson of the North Castle Historical Society; and IBM, Armonk.

North Salem: Richard DeFrances, North Salem Historian; Natalie Hammond of the Hammond Museum; and Ruth Keeler. *Ossining:* Virginia Heill, Ossining Historian; Margaret Brennan and Greta Cornell of the Ossining Historical Society; Margaret Finne, Briarcliff Manor Historian; Barbara Dollard of the Briarcliff Manor/Scarborough Historical Society; Peoples Westchester Savings Bank, Briarcliff Manor; King's College, Briarcliff Manor; and Frank B. Hall, Inc., Briarcliff Manor. *Peekskill:* Norman Kropf, Peekskill Historian; Colin Naylor, former Peekskill Historian; Helen Varian and Thelma Albertson of the Van Cortlandtville Historical Society; and Paul Burns of the Field Library.

Pelham: John House, Pelham Historian; Barbara Bartlett of the Pelham Historical Society; Pelham Public Library; and the *Pelham Sun. Pound Ridge:* Ethel Scofield, Pound Ridge Historian. *Rye:* Elizabeth Witt of the Rye Historical Society; Port Chester Public Library; Rye Free Reading Room; and Frank Ledermann of the Museum of Cartoon Art, Port Chester, *Scarsdale:* Richard Lederer, Jr., Scarsdale Historian; Scarsdale Public Library; Elizabeth Betts of the Scarsdale Historical Society; Joan Bennett, Roberta Peters; and Robert Merrill. *Somers:* Florence Oliver, Somers Historian; and Betsy Wagner of the Somers Historical Society.

White Plains: Renoda Hoffman, White Plains Historian; Richard Maass, County Historian; Ruth Green of the White Plains Public Library; Lowell Schulman; General Foods Corporation; and the Westchester County Dept. of Parks, Recreation, and Conservation. *Yonkers:* Tristram Metcalfe, Yonkers Historian; Lynn Addison of the Hudson River Museum; and Mary Dougal of Philipse Manor Hall.

Outside of Westchester County we received pictures and assistance from Lloyd Ultan, Bronx County Historian; Candace Kuhta of the Bronx County Historical Society; the International Garden Club, Bronx; the Long Island Historical Society, Brooklyn; and the Old Print Shop, New York.

John Kennedy of Yonkers copied hundreds of old photographs, and his talent brought sharpness and clarity to many dim and faded pictures. Francis Falkenbury of Hartsdale, Lindsay H. Welling, Jr., of Armonk, Ira Finke of Mount Kisco, Barbara Novich of Ardsley, and others also copied photographs for us.

We have been especially pleased to work with the National Bank of Westchester on the book. Nancy Hartford, Public Relations Officer at NBW, has counseled and assisted us, and we appreciate both her help and friendship.

Typing and secretarial help has been provided by Edith Mahler of White Plains, Joan Williams of Hastings-on-Hudson, and Megan Swanson of Pelham.

We owe a special debt of gratitude to our husbands and children, who supported and encouraged us throughout the past months. Their advice, as well as their patience, is greatly appreciated.

We feel that the large number of people who contributed to the production of our book makes the volume truly a community effort. We hope Westchester residents will enjoy reading *Westchester County: A Pictorial History* as much as we have enjoyed writing it.

Susan Cochran Swanson
Elizabeth Green Fuller

**Detail from Adriaen Van der Donck's Map
of the New Netherlands, 1656
From Van der Donck's *A Description of the
New Netherlands***

Chapter 1

Pre-History to 1783:
Colonial Westchester and the Revolution

Westchester County covers an area just over 457 square miles. Its geographical setting is a favorable one, with Long Island Sound on the east and the Hudson River on the west. The terrain is largely rolling hills, intersected by three main streams—the Croton, Bronx, and Saw Mill rivers. The county is one of the most heavily forested in New York State. It has retained much of its rural character while adopting the urban and suburban lifestyles dictated by its proximity to New York.

European exploration of the region began with the voyages of Verrazano in 1524 and of Hudson in 1609. Both these explorers were simply looking for a water route to Asia. But the beauty and rich resources found by the early explorers soon brought other Europeans to settle in the area. The abundance of wildlife, particularly beaver, drew many settlers to Westchester. As Westchester's earliest historian, Adriaen Van der Donck, wrote, "Eighty thousand beaver are annually killed in this quarter of the country, besides elk, bears, otters, deer and other animals" (Van der Donck, *A Description of the New Netherlands*). Some Europeans did their own trapping, but most traded blankets, hatchets, glass beads, and other merchandise for beaver trapped by the local Indians. One of the most successful of these early traders was the Dutchman Jan Peek, for whom the city of Peekskill is named.

The Indians of Westchester were members of the Algonkian tribes. They were generally more peace-loving than the fierce Iroquois, who lived in northern New York. They lived on the bounty of their land. They hunted and fished, and grew crops of corn, beans, and pumpkins. Following the seasons, they spent the summers on the shores of the Long Island Sound and Hudson River, and moved to inland homesites during the colder months. They gathered oysters and other shellfish in summer to be smoked and dried to add to their winter food supply.

The seventeenth-century explorers and settlers found several Indian villages in Westchester. They described the Indians they saw as "well proportioned....Their limbs are properly formed, and they are sprightly and active" (Van der Donck, *A Description of the New Netherlands*). They had straight black hair, dark eyes, and swarthy skins. They had strong physical constitutions and were rarely deformed or sickly.

The first permanent white settlers of Westchester County were Dutch, who, in the middle decades of the seventeenth century, began to occupy the Hudson Valley between their earlier settlements in New Amsterdam (now New York) and Fort Orange (now Albany).

Settlement was sponsored by the Dutch West India Company. It became especially attractive after 1638, when William Kieft was appointed director-general of the Dutch colony, and the company liberalized the conditions of colonization, giving anyone the right to hold land, even foreigners. Kieft began acquiring land in what is now Westchester and the Bronx in 1639, and the area soon began to be settled and developed.

Conflict with the Indians arose almost immediately. The Indians sold about twenty-five tracts of land during the colonial period, but they had no conception of property ownership comparable to that of Europeans. In their view, they "owned" the land of Westchester simply by living on it. When the white men offered knives, tools, clothing and blankets, iron kettles, tobacco, beer, and rum in return for land, they expected exclusive possession. The Indians were not really aware of what they were giving up until it was too late.

Adriaen Van der Donck
Courtesy of Hudson River Museum, Yonkers

Intermittent warfare between the Indians and the Dutch and English was to continue for several years. The bloodshed was climaxed by John Underhill's raid on an Indian village near present-day Bedford in 1644, effectively crushing Indian resistance. On August 30, 1645, a general peace treaty was signed between the Dutch and Indians of the Hudson Valley area. War casualties, combined with the diseases brought by the Europeans, greatly diminished the Indian population. While Indians remained for years on the lands they had sold, they gradually disappeared. By 1800 there were very few still living in Westchester.

In the 1640s the English began to move west from their New England settlements to occupy land in what is now Westchester and the Bronx. For two decades the English and Dutch struggled for control over the area, but by 1664 the Dutch were forced to surrender the whole New Netherlands colony.

Many of the English colonists came to America seeking religious and economic freedom. The earliest English settlements in Westchester County were the villages of Westchester (later called the Borough of Westchester, and now part of the Bronx), Rye, Mamaroneck, Eastchester, and Bedford. In the 1680s Huguenots, French Protestants who had been persecuted in their homeland, also came to Westchester to find religious freedom.

At the same time that the English towns were being developed, large tracts of Westchester land were being established as so-called "freehold" manors. The manor proprietors could lease land to tenants or sell it to them outright. Although a proprietor was called "lord of the manor," he was not a "Lord" in the sense of British nobility. There were six manors established in Westchester: Pelham, Fordham, Philipsburgh, Morrisania, Cortlandt, and Scarsdale.

The manor owners had to do a good deal more than just collect rents. They were required to build mills for their tenants; to survey lots and provide livestock for the farms; to provide mechanics, millers, boat builders, and, if possible, a doctor, a clergyman, and a schoolmaster.

Caleb Heathcote, lord of the manor of Scarsdale, was also one of the proprietors of what were called the Three Great Patents. Most patents were tracts of land granted to groups of associates, rather than individuals, to develop through lease or sale. Tenant families on both manor and patent usually held their land for generations.

Strang House, Yorktown, a Rochambeau Headquarters
Courtesy of Westchester County Historical Society

On November 1, 1683, the county of Westchester was created by an act of the New York General Assembly. The county at this time was still largely wilderness, and the life of its settlers was primitive. Nearly everything they consumed was raised or made on their farms. Grains, vegetables, fruits, and livestock were the chief products. Flax was an important crop, and every home had its spinning wheels for the making of linen and wool thread. Wood, cattle, and food were bartered for the necessary items that could not be produced at home.

There were only a few roads in colonial Westchester, and they were very poor. The best means of transportation was by water. Sloops on the Hudson River and Long Island Sound carried a brisk traffic of both passengers and produce, but people living in the interior were quite isolated. In the villages, town meetings were important occasions, and in settlements both large and small, the church was the center of community life. Colonial churches not only served as religious centers, but also played an important social and political role.

The eighteenth century brought some advancement in the standard of living. The lords of the manors lived extremely well, and their tenants, as well as the small independent landowners, gradually improved their homes and land. Some local cottage industries developed in the area, particularly shoemaking and the crafting of furniture. Roads began to be improved, and ferries and taverns established, as travel became more common.

By 1775 Westchester was the richest and most populous county in the colony of New York. It was still almost entirely farmland, dotted with small villages at crossroads and on the waterways. Westchester farmers did not riot over taxes as their neighbors in the New England colonies did; British markets and protected prices for agricultural products were of more importance to them.

Once the Revolution began, however, Westchester saw more fighting and suffering than any other area in the country. From 1776, when Washington and his troops retreated through Westchester after their defeat on Long Island, until 1783, when the British were finally expelled, the county was a battleground. For Westchester, the Revolution was truly a civil war, as families were often divided between patriot and loyalist sympathies.

After the Battles of Pelham and White Plains in October 1776, the main American headquarters was at Continental Village, just north of Peekskill. The British headquarters was in New York City. Westchester became the "Neutral Ground" between the two camps. During the entire course of the war, farmers and townspeople throughout Westchester were subjected to raiding, pillaging, and destruction by both British and American irregulars.

The capture of Major John André, the British spy, by three Westchester men, was an important factor in America's ultimate victory, for it saved West Point, the fortress protecting the Hudson River, from seizure by the British. Westchester also saw the French troops, commanded by Rochambeau, pass along its roads as they came from Rhode Island to help Washington's army defeat the British at Yorktown in 1781.

In 1783, after seven years of suffering, Westchester's countryside was devastated and its population depleted. Recovery from the war would take time and hard work. ■

Balanced Rock, North Salem

The Balanced Rock in North Salem is evidence of the glacial deposits which are an important factor in the geography of Westchester. Composed of a type of red granite found in abundance in Canada and New Hampshire, the rock has been estimated to weigh between sixty and ninety tons. It rests on the points of five smaller rocks of limestone. The glacier, which brought this rock and many more from the far North, carved deep valleys north to south in Westchester, along which many of the county's rivers flow. As a result, crossing the county from east to west has always been difficult, and early settlement generally followed the north to south line of the rivers.

The land on which the boulder sits was donated to the town of North Salem by George Cable. The building behind the rock is the former garage of the Cable family. Photograph by Janet Wilkins; courtesy of Westchester County Historical Society

Henry Hudson's *Half Moon*

In 1609 Henry Hudson, an English explorer hired by the Dutch East India Company to find a northwest passage to India, sailed westward in the Half Moon with a crew of about twenty men. The ship touched Cape Cod on August 3, proceeded to Virginia to visit Hudson's friend John Smith, and then turned north and anchored off present-day Yonkers on September 2. Although sighted by Verrazano in 1524, the Hudson River was not explored before September 11, 1609, when the Half Moon continued its voyage northward. Hudson found the area "as pleasant a land as one need tread upon," but when he had gotten as far as the site of Albany, he realized this was not the long-sought passage to the East.

Hudson had difficulty with his crew on this voyage, partly because he spoke no Dutch. On his fourth voyage, in 1610, after discovering Hudson Bay in Canada, the crew mutinied, and Hudson was set adrift with a few loyal sailors, one of whom was his son. None of them was ever seen again. Courtesy of Hudson River Museum, Yonkers

The Algonkian-speaking Indians were organized loosely into groups, or confederacies, each under the leadership of one strong band or tribe. Most Westchester Indian tribes belonged to the Wappinger Confederacy. The Weckquaesgeeks occupied the area that is now Yonkers, Greenburgh, and Mount Pleasant. The Sint Sinks controlled the land that includes present-day Ossining and Briarcliff Manor. The Kitchawank also lived on the Hudson, from Croton Point to Peekskill, and eastward to Connecticut. The Siwanoys occupied the largest tract in what is now Westchester, living along the north shore of Long Island Sound from New York to Connecticut, and inland at least as far as White Plains. From Ritchie, Indian History of New York State: Part III—the Algonkian Tribes

Wigwam at Trailside Museum, Ward Pound Ridge Reservation

Indian dwellings in Westchester were typically constructed by planting a circle of poles in the ground, then bending them toward the center and lashing their tops together. This framework was further strengthened with poles lashed on horizontally, and then covered with bark or thatched with reeds. A hole was left in the center for smoke to escape. Inside, a circular bench around the walls was used for sitting and sleeping.

The Indians built their houses in both circular and oblong shapes. The longhouses ranged in length from 20 to 100 feet and served as shelter for several families with a number of fires. The modern reconstruction of a round wigwam pictured here is located at the Delaware Indian Resource Center at Trailside Museum in Ward Pound Ridge Reservation.

The Indians also sometimes occupied caves. Finch's Rock House, the best-known cave in this area, is located east of Bedford Road on Windmill Farm in Armonk. It was excavated by the Museum of Natural History in 1901. Photograph by Susan Swanson

Indian artifacts, Trailside Museum, Ward Pound Ridge Reservation. Photograph by Susan Swanson

15

Chief Gramatan

The members of the Algonkian tribes probably had no formal clan organization but instead grouped together by extended biological family, with several generations sharing a longhouse. Several such extended families, banded together, constituted a village. The village was led by a chief or sachem, who was the elder of one of the families. The office was passed through the generations of the family, like a European title of nobility.

There was also a tribal sachem who presided over a group of chieftaincies. Chief Gramatan, shown here in a drawing by Charles R. Knight, was the sachem who turned his lands over to Thomas Pell, first lord of the manor of Pelham. Indian names still abound in Westchester. Gramatan, Katonah, Chappaqua, Sing Sing, and many others currently used testify to the early domination of Westchester by the red man. Courtesy of Bronxville Public Library

**Ho Kohongus Council Tree,
North Tarrytown**

This magnificent chestnut tree, standing more than 100 feet tall, was for many years an awesome sight just across Broadway from the Old Dutch Church of Sleepy Hollow in North Tarrytown. Named Ho Kohongus by the Weckquaesgeek Indians who lived nearby, the tree was believed to be a supernatural being and was the site of the Indians' yearly wheat ceremony. An Indian fort stood on the hill where the Old Dutch Church was later built. After standing for hundreds of years, the tree finally died and was taken down in the early part of the twentieth century. Courtesy of Westchester County Historical Society

Jonas Bronck Treaty

The first white settler on Westchester land was Jonas Bronck, born in Denmark but married to a Dutch woman. Bronck arrived in New Amsterdam in 1639 and purchased from the Indians 500 acres of land between the Harlem and Aquehung (now Bronx) rivers. In this picture he is shown signing a peace treaty with his Indian neighbors in 1642, in the first house built by white hands on Westchester County soil. This treaty brought an end to a war between the Dutch settlers and the Indians, which had resulted from the murder, in 1641, of a Dutch trader in Manhattan by an Indian warrior. The Indian was in turn avenging the murder of his uncle by a white man many years earlier. Unfortunately, despite the treaty, bloodshed would soon begin again.

Bronck died in 1643; it is not known whether he was killed by Indians. His widow remarried and moved away. Courtesy of Huguenot-Thomas Paine Historical Association, New Rochelle

Ann Hutchinson

John Underhill

Ann Hutchinson was born Ann Marbury in 1591, in Lincolnshire, England. She married Will Hutchinson, and in 1634 they left England with their children to make a new home in America. Ann had radical religious views for her day. She believed that God spoke directly to her, and she organized groups of women to study and talk together about their religion. Her views angered the Puritan fathers, but when she confessed "wrong thinking," they agreed to admit her into the Massachusetts Bay Colony. Her religious practices continued, however, and in 1637 she was brought to trial by Governor John Winthrop, who banished her from the colony. John Throgmorton and Thomas Cornell, who tried to help her, were also banished.

The group went to Rhode Island to live in Roger Williams's colony there; but, in 1642 Will Hutchinson died, and in 1643 Ann moved on. With a group of sixteen friends and family members, she settled in the Eastchester area, near where her old friends Throgmorton and Cornell were already living. The exact site of her house has been disputed for many years, but in any event she did not live there long. In August 1643 Indians killed Ann and all her companions, except for her youngest daughter, Susannah, who was taken captive. Courtesy of Westchester County Historical Society

John Underhill made his reputation by fighting to control Indian raiding parties like the one which murdered Ann Hutchinson. He had come to the Massachusetts Bay Colony in 1630 and soon rose to a position of prominence as a commander during the Pequot War. Underhill, however, supported the cause of Ann Hutchinson and her family, and like her was banished from the Massachusetts Bay Colony. He returned to England for a time. By 1642 he was back again in the colonies, serving as military commander in Stamford, Connecticut.

New Indian uprisings were feared throughout the colonies. Worried that if the Indians were victorious on Long Island and in New Amsterdam, other tribes would go on the warpath, Governor William Kieft of New Amsterdam hired Underhill to help deal with the problem. Underhill's first victory was on Long Island in early 1644. Shortly thereafter, Underhill was in northern Westchester with a force of about 130 men. Under cover of darkness, the Dutch attacked an Indian village located near what is now Bedford. After killing more than 180 Indians in battle, the soldiers set fire to their lodges, and hundreds more perished in the flames. The soldiers were amazed that throughout the inferno not a single shriek or moan was heard. Between 500 and 700 Indians died that night, and only about a dozen soldiers were killed or wounded.

This massacre ended a five-year war in which over 1,600 Indians were killed. John Underhill lived the remainder of his life on Long Island and died in 1672. Courtesy of Westchester County Historical Society

Attack on Van der Donck's Home

Adriaen Van der Donck was the first, and only, patroon in Westchester. He was the first lawyer in the New Netherlands and had served as sheriff for Killiaen Van Rensselaer, the patroon of Rensselaerwyck. In 1646 Van der Donck purchased from the Indians a sixteen-mile section of land in what was to become Westchester. He spent only three years there as a patroon on his farm, Colen Donck, before traveling to Holland to plead the cause of the settlers who were dissatisfied with the governorship of Peter Stuyvesant in New Amsterdam.

For three years Van der Donck was refused permission by Stuyvesant to return to his home in America. While in Holland, he wrote a history of the New Netherlands, which is the most comprehensive source of information available on the Dutch colony. Finally, in 1653, the Dutch government allowed Van der Donck to return to America, and Stuyvesant was called back to Holland to account for his management of the colony. Van der Donck came back to his farm and sawmill. This mill was to give the Saw Mill River its name.

Van der Donck died two years later, probably before the Indians attacked his home in September 1655. Here the attack is shown in a painting by John Ward Dunsmore. In the fight, three farmhands were killed, and a young girl was kidnapped by the Indians. Van der Donck's widow, who inherited Colen Donck, later remarried, and eventually the land was sold. A part of the property was bought by John Archer, who established Fordham Manor. Courtesy of Westchester County Historical Society

In 1654 Thomas Pell purchased 9,000 acres of land from the Siwanoy Indians. The area included what is today the Pelhams, New Rochelle, City Island, and part of the Bronx. This was the manor of Pelham, and it opened the whole area to settlement. Later 6,000 acres of the original Pell purchase were sold to the Huguenots.

The house shown here, which stands on the boundary line between Pelham Manor and New Rochelle on Pelham Road, was built in 1761. It is a typical colonial farmhouse, built by Joshua Pell II, a Loyalist during the Revolution and a grandson of Thomas Pell II, third lord of Pelham Manor. The property originally consisted of about 250 acres of shore front, including Hunter's Island, Travers Island, and David's Island. After the Revolution, Pell fled to Nova Scotia, and his property was bought by William Bayley, whose wife was the daughter of Joseph Pell, fourth lord of Pelham Manor. Mother Elizabeth Seton, a niece of the Bayleys, spent several summers in the house as a child. The house has since had several owners and is still a private residence. Courtesy of Westchester County Historical Society

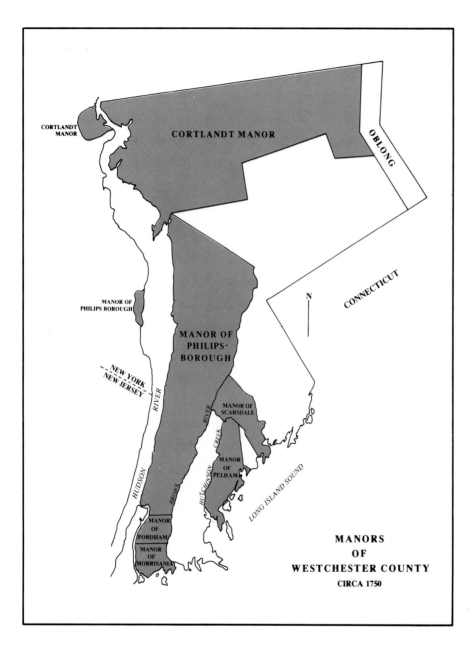

The Manors of Westchester

Manors constituted the major portion of Westchester County until the Revolution. There were six manors: Pelham (1666), Fordham (1671), Philipsburgh (1693), Morrisania (1697), Cortlandt (1697), and Scarsdale (1701). The Three Great Patents were granted to Caleb Heathcote and his associates in 1701; the last of the great patents (the Oblong) was granted to twenty-five men from Ridgefield, Connecticut, in 1709. Map by Barbara Bartlett; after Scharf, History of Westchester County

Joshua Pell House, Pelham Manor

Philipse Manor Hall, Yonkers

Philipse Manor Hall was the home of Frederick Philipse (in Dutch, Vredryk Vlypse), who became lord of the second largest manor in Westchester in 1693. Philipse began purchasing land in Westchester in 1681 and built his home in 1682 in what is now Yonkers. This house became the social center of the whole Hudson River Valley. Philipse eventually owned 90,000 acres from the Hudson to the Bronx River—land which includes all of present-day Yonkers, Greenburgh, Mount Pleasant, and Ossining, with the exception of Mile Square in Yonkers, which had been sold previously.

The Philipses were Loyalists and lost the whole manor after the Revolution. The Manor Hall had several owners over the years, and as Yonkers grew, the building, shown here as it appeared in the early 1800s, became surrounded by the city. In 1868, it became the first city hall of Yonkers. New York State purchased it from the city in 1908, and today it is a museum. Courtesy of Westchester County Historical Society

Frederick Philipse built two mills on his manor, the Lower Mill in Yonkers and the Upper Mills in what later became North Tarrytown. The Upper Mills served both as a gristmill for his tenant farmers and as a trade depot. Philipse also built a two-story manor house here, simpler than the Manor Hall in Yonkers.

When Frederick Philipse died in 1702, his son Adolph inherited the manor and increased the capacity of the Upper Mills by adding a third set of grindstones so that barley could be ground as well as wheat and corn. Note that the mill wheel is undershot, that is, the water runs under the wheel to push the paddles around as the water flows past.

The entire manor was built up under Adolph's direction; the tenant population increased from 200 in 1702 to 1,100 in 1750. When Adolph died in 1750, leaving no will, his nephew, Frederick Philipse II, inherited the manor. This lord was more interested in law and politics than in agriculture, as was his son, Frederick III, who inherited the manor in 1751. He leased the Upper Mills to William Pugsley to operate. Frederick Philipse III sided with the Crown when the Revolution began, and the entire manor was confiscated by the state of New York and sold after the war.

The Upper Mills property was bought by Gerard G. Beekman, Jr., who added a wing to the manor house. During the nineteenth and early twentieth centuries, the manor house had several owners. The property was abandoned during the Depression and fell into disrepair.

In 1937 the Historical Society of the Tarrytowns, hoping to save the Upper Mills, approached John D. Rockefeller, Jr., for help. He purchased the property in 1940, and it was restored and opened to the public in 1943. In 1951 it became part of the Sleepy Hollow Restorations, a non-profit organization established by Rockefeller, and a new restoration was begun. The added wing on the manor house was removed and the house and mill restored to their mid-eighteenth century appearance. *Courtesy of Sleepy Hollow Restorations*

Old Dutch Church, North Tarrytown

The most serious problem that plagued the Upper Mills was the repeated washing away of the dam on the Pocantico River. According to legend, one of the slaves on the manor dreamed that the problem would continue until there was a church on the estate. Upon hearing this, Frederick Philipse gave top priority to the construction of a church, and it was completed in 1685. Whether or not the slave's dream was true, the dam held after the church was built!

The Old Dutch Church was formally organized as a congregation in 1697, and is believed to be the oldest extant church in New York State. By 1854 the congregation, which had outgrown its little church, built a more centrally located First Reformed Church on North Broadway in the center of North Tarrytown. The Old Dutch Church has never had heat or electricity, but it is still used by the First Reformed Church for services in July and August. It is located on Broadway in North Tarrytown, just across from the Upper Mills of Philipsburgh Manor. Courtesy of Sleepy Hollow Restorations

Hammond House, Valhalla

Typical of the farmhouses constructed on Philipsburgh Manor is the Hammond House, built in 1719 by Colonel William Hammond. He built the house without a cellar, so that it could be moved if his lease were terminated at a later date.

The present structure has three sections, the central part being the original house. The left-hand section was once a separate cottage, which was joined to the older house around 1835; the right-hand section was probably added in the 1860s.

Colonel Hammond was an active member of the manor community and an elder of the Old Dutch Church. His son, James, inherited the lease to the property in 1762. He was active in the Revolution, serving as lieutenant colonel of the First Regiment of Westchester Militia from August 1776 until the end of the war, except when he was held captive by the British for a year and a half.

After the war Colonel Hammond bought the land which his family had previously leased from Philipsburgh Manor. He and subsequent generations of the Hammond family occupied the house until 1832. The house was acquired by the Westchester County Historical Society in 1926 and has been restored as a typical farm home of the Revolutionary period. Located on Grasslands Road, Route 100-C, in Valhalla, the Hammond House is open to the public. Courtesy of Westchester County Historical Society

Hammond House, Kitchen

The main rooms of the Hammond House have been furnished and equipped with items known to have been in use in the period from 1750 to 1800. The kitchen was the heart of the colonial home. Imagine a blazing fire in the fireplace, with a delicious aroma coming from the bubbling pot hanging on the swinging crane. The bake oven and warming closet can also be seen in this picture. Courtesy of Westchester County Historical Society

Sherwood House, Yonkers

The Sherwood House, located at 340 Tuckahoe Road, is the second oldest house remaining in Yonkers. (The oldest is Philipse Manor Hall.) It was built by Stephen Sherwood, a tenant on the Philipsburgh Manor, around 1740. After the Revolution, the Sherwoods were able to purchase house and land, just as the Hammonds and many other tenants purchased their properties.

From 1834 until 1923, the house was owned by Frederick Weed, who operated a tavern in it, and his descendants. The house is well-constructed, built into a steep hillside and possessing a stone basement. Its two-story porch with curving roof suggests the Dutch influence so prevalent in lower Westchester.

The house was owned for a time by Dr. John Ingersoll, the first physician in the area. Eventually, Consolidated Edison acquired the property and planned to demolish the house but instead gave it to the Yonkers Historical Society, which has restored it and opened it to the public. *Courtesy of Westchester County Historical Society*

Rent Receipt, Philipsburgh Manor

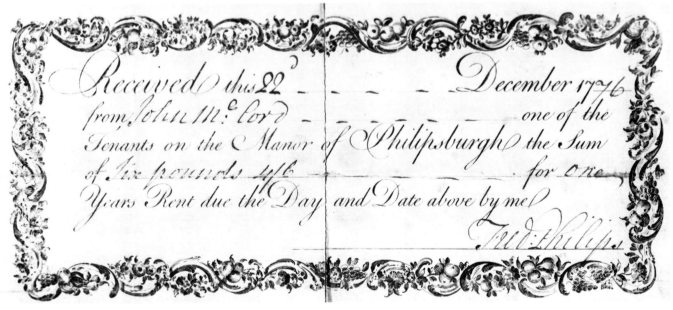

The lords of Philipsburgh Manor received fixed rents from their tenants for the use of their land. "Rent days" were held twice a year at Yonkers and Sleepy Hollow and were enjoyable social events on the manor. Tenants paid as little as two hens or a bushel of wheat, or as much as several pounds sterling, depending on the value of the land they leased. The lord of the manor provided a good dinner on rent day, and the tenants enjoyed the opportunity to exchange news and gossip with their neighbors. *Courtesy of Westchester County Historical Society*

Van Cortlandt Manor House, Croton

Even larger than Philipsburgh Manor was the Cortlandt Manor on the Hudson River to the north. In only two years' time, between 1677 and 1679, Stephanus Van Cortlandt acquired holdings of nearly 200 square miles. In 1697 he became the first and only lord of the manor of Cortlandt. He died in 1700 and willed his land to all his immediate heirs, rather than to his eldest son alone. His New York City home, the manor house in Croton, and 10,000 acres were left to the eldest son, Philip Van Cortlandt. When Philip died in 1747, the manor house became the home of his son, Pierre Van Cortlandt, the first of the family to make it his permanent home. Merchant, politician, and patriot, he presided over the convention in 1777 that drafted the first constitution for the state of New York.

During the Revolution, the family moved for safety to the Upper Manor House, in Van Cortlandtville. Pierre's son, Philip, served in the American army during the war. When peace returned, the manor life resumed, and Philip rebuilt the manor house, which had been damaged by the British. Philip died in 1831, and the house remained in the Van Cortlandt family until 1945.

In 1953 John D. Rockefeller, Jr., acquired the property and had it restored to its late eighteenth-century form. Along with Philipse Manor Upper Mills and Washington Irving's Sunnyside, which appears later in this book, it is one of the Sleepy Hollow Restorations. Photograph by Tom Leonard; courtesy of Sleepy Hollow Restorations

Van Cortlandt Manor Dining Room

The dining room at Van Cortlandt Manor has been restored to the post-Revolutionary period, showing more of the later, English influence than the pre-Revolutionary Dutch. The Dutch tiles around the fireplace are original to the house. Each tile depicts a scene from the Old Testament. The monteith bowl on the table was made in Delft, Holland, in 1700 and was used for chilling and washing wine glasses. Courtesy of Sleepy Hollow Restorations

Bethel Chapel, Croton

Since Pierre Van Cortlandt was a patriot, he did not lose his land after the Revolution and continued his beneficies to the local community. Bethel Chapel is believed to have been built around 1780 on land given to the village of Croton by Van Cortlandt. It came under the supervision of the Methodist Society in 1831 and was used by the Methodists until they moved into the Asbury Church in 1883. Bethel Chapel was one of the stops for the early Methodist circuit riders.

The church has suffered several fires during its long history and was reconstructed and rededicated in 1936. Its organ is thought to be one of the oldest in the United States. Photograph by Julianna FreeHand

Richbell's Land Purchase, Mamaroneck

Prior to the formation of the manors of Philipsburgh and Cortlandt, John Richbell purchased three large tracts of land from the Indians in 1661. He then applied to the Dutch Crown for a patent on his purchase, which lay between present-day Rye and Pelham and extended inland to what is now White Plains, Scarsdale, and the southern part of New Castle.

There is a strong suspicion that Richbell served as a business front for smugglers. In 1657 he had formed a partnership in Barbados with two other men, who sent him to the American colonies "to inform himself about the coast and islands between Connecticut and the Dutch colony, to pick a plantation 'near a navigable stream,' and to find out whether the government was 'strict or remisse'" (Crandell, This Is Westchester).

Richbell was not successful in his attempt to develop the land he purchased. When he died in 1684, his widow sold what was left of the original purchase to various settlers.

The scene depicted here is a re-enactment of Richbell's purchase from the Indians in 1661. The occasion was the celebration of the 300th anniversary of the town of Mamaroneck, in 1961. Courtesy of Westchester County Historical Society

Caleb Heathcote

The last of the Westchester manors to be formed was Scarsdale in 1701. Caleb Heathcote, who arrived in America in 1697, wasted no time in getting involved in local politics and becoming mayor of the Borough of Westchester. He began acquiring land for his manor by buying the remainder of John Richbell's land from his widow. Heathcote then bought the land between the headwaters of the Hutchinson and Bronx rivers and built himself a large brick manor house overlooking Mamaroneck Harbor.

In addition to his land holdings in the manor of Scarsdale, Heathcote bought, with several associates, almost all the interior of the county between Cortlandt Manor on the north, Philipsburgh Manor on the west, White Plains and Harrison's Purchase on the south, and Connecticut on the east. This land was known as the Three Great Patents and comprised about 70,000 acres. The land was gradually sold or leased to individual settlers. Photograph from Scharf, History of Westchester County

Landing of the Huguenots, New Rochelle

Huguenot Church, New Rochelle

*Since the search for religious freedom motivated
the settlement of Huguenots in America and the
subsequent founding of New Rochelle, it is not
surprising that one of the first buildings
constructed in New Rochelle was a church. The
first building, made of wood, was built in 1692.
It was replaced in 1711 by the building shown
here, a small square building constructed of
wood and field stone which stood on Huguenot
Street. The Huguenots were so anxious to have
it finished that even the women helped, carrying
stones and mortar to the site in their aprons.*

*During the Revolution, the church was first
used as a storage house for salt belonging to the
state and then, during the British occupation of
New Rochelle in October 1776, as a prison for
captured Americans. The little building was
once again used as a place of worship after the
war, but was torn down in 1793 to make way for
the Boston Post Road. Courtesy of Westchester
County Historical Society*

Protestants in France were long persecuted for their religious beliefs. The Edict of Nantes, in 1598, was supposed to guarantee their religious freedom, but it was revoked in 1685. Thereafter French Protestants, or Huguenots, as they were known, suffered more than ever and began to leave France in great numbers. Many went to England and other European countries, but gradually a number found their way to New York.

The French Huguenots who settled in Westchester landed at Bonnefoy's Point, on the eastern part of Davenport Neck in New Rochelle. They were determined to stay together in order to maintain their language and customs. There were other Huguenot settlements, notably at New Paltz, New York, but the Westchester group retained its French character far longer than the rest.

In 1689 Jacob Leisler, a wealthy Huguenot merchant living in New York City, purchased from John Pell 6,000 acres of land for the Huguenots. This land they called New Rochelle, since many of them had emigrated from La Rochelle in France. It represented two-thirds of the manor of Pelham, and the price was £ 1,625, plus a yearly rent of "one fatte calfe."

Leisler usurped the duties of lieutenant governor of New York in 1689, and in 1691 the English Crown sent Henry Sloughter to take Leisler's place. Although Leisler surrendered his command peaceably, he was arrested and tried for treason. He and his son-in-law were executed, the only people ever executed in New York State for political crimes. Five years after their deaths, Leisler and his son-in-law were both pardoned by an act of Parliament. A statue of Leisler in New Rochelle commemorates the service he performed for his fellow Huguenots. Courtesy of Westchester County Historical Society

Allaire House, New Rochelle

The early Huguenot stone houses, of which the Allaire house was a typical example, were similar in construction and design to the French homes from which the Huguenots had been forced to flee. These houses usually contained one main story plus a loft. The Allaires were one of the founding families of New Rochelle, and their house was probably built shortly after their arrival. The house stood on the south side of the Boston Post Road (now Huguenot Street) and was demolished some time before 1938. Courtesy of Huguenot-Thomas Paine Historical Association, New Rochelle

Rye was the second town established in Westchester County. (The Borough of Westchester, now part of the Bronx, was the first.) In 1660 Rye, originally called Hastings, was founded by an organizing company, the members of which were called "proprietors." The proprietors made several purchases of land from the Indians, which, put together, included the present-day towns of Rye and Harrison, and the city of White Plains.

Each proprietor was entitled to a piece of land for himself and to the use of other land held "in common"; such an arrangement was familiar to them from the New England towns they had known earlier.

Kirby Mill, pictured here, was a tide mill built in Rye in 1770 on Long Island Sound. It was operated by David Kirby for fifty years. A pond at the back of the mill filled twice a day as the tide came in. At ebb tide, the pond water, retained by a valve gate, was four or five feet higher than the level of the Sound, so when the miller opened the valve and let the pond empty, the water turned the mill wheel. Five or six hours of grinding could be done with each tide.

The Kirby Tide Mill currently houses the offices of a boat club. Courtesy of Westchester County Historical Society

Kirby Tide Mill, Rye

Bush Homestead, Port Chester

The Bush homestead in Port Chester was built by Justus Bush in the early eighteenth century and was occupied by his descendants for 150 years. Bush, a merchant from New York City, purchased land near Sawpit Landing, as Port Chester was first known, in 1726.

Tradition holds that General Israel Putnam used the house as his headquarters for several months during 1777-1778. A small desk which belonged to Putnam can still be seen in the house. Restored in 1938, the house is now owned by the Park Commission of Port Chester. Located in Lyon Park, it is operated as a museum by the Port Chester Historical Society. Courtesy of Westchester County Historical Society

Bush Slave Quarters, Port Chester

While there were never great numbers of slaves in Westchester, they were a measurable portion of the population in colonial times. The first census in the province of New York, in 1698, showed 917 whites and 146 blacks in the county of Westchester. Most slave holders owned only a few slaves. The Van Cortlandts had ten at their manor house in Croton.

The building pictured here housed the slaves of the Bush family in Port Chester. Courtesy of Westchester County Historical Society

Mott Family Slaves, Larchmont

In this region, slaves were generally employed as house servants. "Uncle Billy" and "Aunt Jinny" served three generations of the Mott family in Larchmont and were beloved of their owners. Jinny, who had been stolen from her African family as a child around 1744, said that her father was a king. Billy, born on Long Island about 1738, was known as "Billy Banjo" because of his skill as a musician. Billy and Jinny were freed in 1770 but remained in the Mott household.

The movement to free slaves began early in New York State. By 1779 the Society of Friends in Westchester had resolved that all Friends' slaves should be freed and that their former owners should help to support them. In 1817 an act was passed by the New York legislature providing for the gradual abolition of all slavery in the state. The final slave, who belonged to the Morris family of Morrisania, was freed in 1827. Photograph from Cornell, Adam and Anne Mott

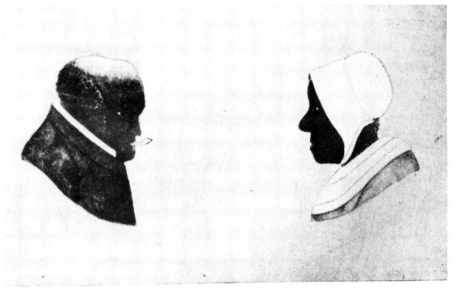

BILLY AND JINNY.
From a Water Color by Robert F. Mott, about 1814.

Bedford Green

The area which became Bedford was acquired by eight separate purchases of land from the Indians, the first in 1680, and the last in 1722. Bedford's settlers followed the New England traditions which they had known in Connecticut, much as the settlers of Rye had done twenty years earlier. They laid out a common of about three acres and assigned individual house and pasture lots by lottery.

The Bedford settlers considered themselves part of the colony of Connecticut, and a subsequent dispute arose between New York and Connecticut over lands in Bedford and in Rye, continuing for seventy years.

This picture of Bedford Green was taken in the early 1900s, when the area was still very much rural and the roads still unpaved. Courtesy of Bedford Historical Society

Matthew's Mill, Bedford

Sawmills to provide lumber for houses and gristmills for grinding crops into meal and flour were essential in the Westchester wilderness. On the manors, the landowners were responsible for establishing mills for their tenants. Matthew's Mill was the second mill in Bedford. It was built in 1701 by agreement of the town with John Dibell and was located on the Beaver Dam River. It was demolished many years ago. Courtesy of Bedford Historical Society

Friends Meeting House, Chappaqua

There were Quakers very early in Westchester, first in the Borough of Westchester (now part of the Bronx), and then at Rye, Mamaroneck, and Harrison where the land John Harrison bought for the Quakers is still known as the "Purchase." Thence, Quaker settlers moved further into central and northern Westchester, in the area between the Dutch settlements on the west and Connecticut on the east.

By 1752 the Chappaqua Society of Friends desired a meeting house of its own. Subscriptions were taken in the Mamaroneck and Oblong Monthly Meetings to help pay for the Chappaqua Meeting House, which was completed in 1753.

During the Revolution, American soldiers wounded at the Battle of White Plains were taken to the Chappaqua Meeting House for treatment and care; wounded British soldiers were cared for at the Harrison Quaker Meeting House.

The Chappaqua Meeting House, on Quaker Road, is the oldest meeting house still standing in the county. The Chappaqua Meeting is still held every week in the original structure. It has had only two additions since 1753; the porch was added in the nineteenth century. Photograph by Gray Williams, Jr.

Construction of the present St. Paul's Church began in 1763, on the site of an earlier wooden church. The new church was not finished when the Revolution began. During the war it was used as a hospital for Hessian soldiers. Work on the building resumed when the war was over, and it was completed in 1787. A gallery was added in 1804.

St. Paul's, as well as other Episcopal churches in Westchester, was supported by a general tax on the entire population, rather than just on members of the congregation. The vestry and wardens were elected by a general vote of all voters, regardless of religion. This meant that Presbyterians, or "Independents," were often members of the governing body of the Episcopal church, a policy which often created problems.

St. Paul's bell, which is rung thirteen times each Fourth of July, was cast in the same foundry as the Liberty Bell in Philadelphia. During the Revolution, the bell and the church silver were buried for safekeeping.

Restoration of St. Paul's was carried out during 1931-1942 by a committee headed by Sara Delano Roosevelt, mother of Franklin Delano Roosevelt. In November 1980 the church was acquired by the U.S. Department of the Interior, to be operated as a National Historic Site. Photograph by Charles Phelps Cushing; courtesy of Westchester County Historical Society

1733 Election Held on Village Green, Eastchester

St. Paul's Church, Eastchester, Mount Vernon

On October 29, 1733, on the Eastchester Green (now the grounds of St. Paul's Church), an election was held which was to be of great historical significance. The vote was to elect a representative from Westchester County to the New York Provincial Assembly. Lewis Morris was the candidate favored by most people, but the royal governor, William Cosby, put up his own candidate in opposition. Moreover, the election notice he prepared specified the date but not the time of the election so that many voters missed it.

At this time, only freeholders owning property worth £40, debt-free, could vote, a rule which excluded tenant farmers, laborers, and men with very small farms. At the election, government officials required proof of land ownership and demanded that voters swear on the Bible that they were giving correct information. A group of Quakers refused to swear, as their religion forbade it, so they were barred from voting.

John Peter Zenger's newspaper, the New York Weekly Journal, first published on November 5, 1733, contained an article criticizing Governor Cosby's conduct of the election. The governor then had Zenger arrested on a charge of seditious libel. After being held in prison for several months, Zenger was brought to trial. His quick acquittal was a verdict which established an important legal precedent for freedom of the press. *Courtesy of Westchester County Historical Society*

33

Keeler Branding Iron, North Salem

While concern over the political situation and the problems created by British rule was growing, Westchester farmers also had to deal with more immediate problems. One of these was the control of domestic animals. Some means of identification of animals grazing on common land or allowed to run loose in the woods was necessary. Branding was a common practice, and records were kept in the towns, listing animals, their owners, and their identifying brands.

The branding iron pictured here belonged to the Keeler family of North Salem. The Keelers were one of the first families to settle in the area; at one time a section of the town was called Keelerville because, as Miss Ruth Keeler, who still lives in North Salem, put it, "there were so many Keelers around." The branding iron, donated by Miss Keeler, is one of the prized possessions of the North Salem Historical Society. Photograph by Susan Swanson

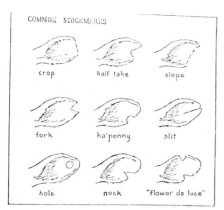

COMMON STOCKMARKS

crop — half take — slope

fork — ha'penny — slit

hole — neck — "flower de luce"

Earmarks

In addition to branding, earmarks were used in colonial times to identify domestic animals. After the Revolution, cities and towns were required by state law to maintain pounds for stray animals. Each town maintained such a pound, and fees had to be paid to the pound master to regain stray animals that had been impounded.

The earmarks shown here were commonly used on cows, sheep, and other animals. Earmarks, like brands, were recorded in town record books. From Lee, **New Castle Historical Records**

Purdy Homestead, North Salem

The Purdy homestead in Purdys, North Salem, was begun on June 17 1775, the date of the Battle of Bunker Hill. Joseph Purdy, who built the house, was the grandson of the first Purdy in Westchester—Francis Purdy, whose sons in the early 1700s acquired 1,000 acres of land that had formerly been part of Cortlandt Manor.

Members of the Purdy family have occupied the house ever since, and several of them have been influential in the history of the county. The Purdy farm is typical of the comfortable lifestyle that had evolved in Westchester by the second half of the eighteenth century. The tranquility of the countryside, however, would not last much longer. Courtesy of North Salem Historical Society

St. Peter's Church, Westchester

Speaking for the local farmers who were against the radical changes being proposed throughout the colonies, Reverend Samuel Seabury, rector of St. Peter's Church in the Borough of Westchester (now part of the Bronx), published a series of pamphlets in 1774. Entitled Letters of a Westchester Farmer, *they strongly opposed the economic sanctions enacted by the First Continental Congress in retaliation for British taxation of the colonies. Seabury's* Letters *reflected the conflict within many Westchester families, who considered themselves patriotic Americans but who did not want to fight a war of separation from England. Courtesy of Westchester County Historical Society*

Reading of the Declaration of Independence, White Plains

On July 1, 1776, the British fleet arrived to occupy New York City. The New York Provincial Congress had fled New York the day before, seeking safety at the Westchester County Court House (located at present-day South Broadway and Mitchell Place) in White Plains. There, on July 9, the Congress unanimously approved the Declaration of Independence, and on July 10 voted that "the title of this house be changed to the Convention of the Representatives of the State of New York." Thus the new state of New York was born at White Plains, which served as the state capital until July 27.

On July 11, John Thomas of Harrison read the Declaration of Independence to the populace from the steps of the Court House. This was the first public reading of the Declaration in the state of New York. This painting of the historic event is by George Albert Harker. *Courtesy of Westchester County Historical Society*

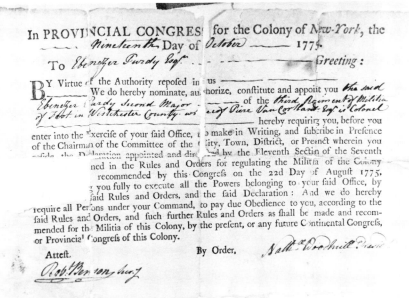

In PROVINCIAL CONGRESS for the Colony of New-York, the Nineteenth Day of October 1775.

To Ebenezer Purdy Esqr. Greeting:

BY Virtue of the Authority reposed in us We do hereby nominate, authorize, constitute and appoint you the said Ebenezer Purdy Second Major of the Third Regiment of Militia of Foot in Westchester County whereof Pierre Van Cortlandt Esqr is Colonel hereby requiring you, before you enter into the exercise of your said Office, to make in Writing, and subscribe in Presence of the Chairman of the Committee of the City, Town, District, or Precinct wherein you reside, the Declaration appointed and directed by the Eleventh Section of the Seventh ned in the Rules and Orders for regulating the Militia of the Colony recommended by this Congress on the 22d Day of August 1775, you fully to execute all the Powers belonging to your said Office, by said Rules and Orders, and the said Declaration: And we do hereby require all Persons under your Command, to pay due Obedience to you, according to the said Rules and Orders, and such further Rules and Orders as shall be made and recommended for the Militia of this Colony, by the present, or any future Continental Congress, or Provincial Congress of this Colony.

Attest.

Rob. Benson, secry

By Order, Nathl. Woodhull Presid

Purdy Commission

Once American blood had been spilled at Lexington and Concord in April 1775, Westchester families were soon forced to commit themselves to one side or the other. The Continental Congress ordered the colonies to raise militias, and many Westchester men received commissions similar to Ebenezer Purdy's, shown here. Three Westchester regiments were created in October 1775, headed by Colonels Pierre Van Cortlandt, Joseph Drake, and John Thomas. The three regiments totaled twenty-eight companies, each of which elected its own officers. A soldier was required to provide for himself a musket, bayonet, sword or tomahawk, cartridge box, knapsack, one pound of gunpowder, twelve flints, and three pounds of musket balls. Courtesy of Westchester County Historical Society

Odell Tavern, Irvington

This little building on the Albany Post Road (now Route 9) in Irvington was built on Philipsburgh Manor in the 1690s by Jan Harmse. It was later used as a tavern by Mathias Conklin and in 1774 was leased by Jonathan Odell for the same purpose. It was in the Odell Tavern that the Committee of Safety, the executive committee of the Convention of Representatives of the State of New York, met on August 31, 1776. They learned grave news that day. General Washington's army had been defeated at the Battle of Long Island. All was not lost, however, since Colonel John Glover and his Marblehead Mariners had successfully evacuated the American troops across the East River to Manhattan.

Jonathan Odell later became one of the Westchester Guides, who were civilian scouts for the American army. Nineteen other local young men also risked their lives many times over as Guides, helping the patriots' cause.

In 1785 Jonathan Odell purchased the tavern property from the Commissioners of Forfeiture, who were responsible for disposing of the confiscated Philipsburgh Manor property. Odell continued to operate the tavern until 1818. It has had many owners since and is still in private hands. Courtesy of Irvington Historical Society

*This nineteenth-century etching depicts
Valentine's Hill (which now overlooks the
Cross County Shopping Center) in Yonkers as
it probably looked in October 1776. American
troops moved to the hill when General Howe
attempted to invade the mainland at Throg's
Neck (now in the Bronx) on October 12, 1776.
The fierce rifle fire of twenty-five Americans
hidden behind a huge woodpile at Westchester,
near St. Peter's Church, overwhelmed the
musketfire of the British, causing Howe to halt
and wait for reinforcements.*

*That night, when the tide rushed up West-
chester Creek, Howe found himself stranded on
Throg's Neck "island." Furious that he had not
reached the mainland, he took the advice of his
Tory guide, Joshua Pell of Pelham Manor, and
moved his army to land at Pell's Point, at the
mouth of the Hutchinson River.*

*Howe's objective was to reach the Boston Post
Road and cut off Washington's supply route
from New England. He planned to march west
along the Post Road, attack Washington's
troops from the rear at King's Bridge, and with
British naval support on the East and North
(Hudson) rivers, surround and annihilate the
American army. Courtesy of Westchester
County Historical Society*

Colonel John Glover

Split Rock, Pelham

*With the British located at Throg's Neck,
Washington knew he had to evacuate his army
from Manhattan. On October 18, 1776, he
ordered his soldiers to start moving toward
safety at White Plains.*

*Washington posted Colonel John Glover and
750 men to protect the vital bridge over the
Hutchinson River on the Boston Post Road at
East Chester. Glover's "web-footed regiments"
were made up of sailors and fishermen from
Marblehead, Salem, and Woburn, Massachusetts. They had proved their worth by evacu-
ating the American army from Long Island
after the British victory there in August.*

*At dawn on the eighteenth, Glover climbed a
ridge and trained his glass on Pelham Bay.
There he saw 200 British ships landing 4,000
troops. The British had finally reached the
mainland. Courtesy of Westchester County
Historical Society*

*Colonel Glover placed his three small regiments
in ambush behind the stone walls of Split Rock
Road. As the British advanced, they encoun-
tered fire so fierce that they broke and ran back
to Pell's Point. Howe later testified that he
thought he was being opposed by Washington's
main force.*

*Fighting raged for several hours, until Glover
was attacked by Cornwallis from the rear. He
retreated over the Hutchinson River, destroying
the Post Road Bridge as he went. The British
did not follow but camped along the Post Road
in Pelham and New Rochelle until October 25.*

*The heroic action of Glover's 750 men
allowed Washington enough time to move the
American army safely to White Plains. The
Battle of Pelham, though small, has become
recognized as one of the most significant of the
Revolution. Split Rock, the site of the battle,
remains in Pelham, located between the
Hutchinson River Parkway and the New
England Thruway. Courtesy of Westchester
County Historical Society*

While the British were camped in Pelham and New Rochelle, Washington completed the movement of his army to White Plains. Finally, on October 28, Howe moved his army north to confront the American troops. Howe had slightly fewer men, but they were battle veterans with the best of equipment and supplies. Washington's men were inexperienced and inadequately armed.

The American forces, poorly dug in on Chatterton Hill (sometimes referred to as Battle Hill), must have looked down at the advancing British troops in awe. As Captain William Hull described the British army:

Its appearance was truly magnificent. A bright autumnal sun shed its full lustre on the polished arms; and the rich array of dress and military equipage gave an imposing grandeur to the scene, as they advanced in all the pomp and circumstance of war to give us battle (Hufeland, Westchester County During the American Revolution).

The resulting battle did not last long! The redcoats charged up Chatterton Hill. The ill-trained American militia broke and fled. The somewhat more seasoned Continental troops fought bravely and repulsed several attacks from the east, across the Bronx River. They were forced to fall back, however, when they were flanked from the west. The battle lasted only fifteen minutes; the Americans suffered 175 casualties and the British 229.

The British dug in on Chatterton Hill and made no attempt to pursue the Americans. Howe planned to attack Washington again on October 31, but a rainstorm caused him to delay until November 1. Washington outsmarted him, however. During Howe's three-days' delay, Washington moved his lines into the rugged North Castle hills where they were secure from attack. Although Howe is credited with a victory at White Plains, the Americans gained time by the encounter, and the taste of battle seasoned the inexperienced troops. Moreover, Washington's military finesse had helped to save the American forces, now more determined than ever to fight on. Courtesy of Westchester County Historical Society

Thomas Paine Cottage, New Rochelle

The Jacob Purdy house in White Plains was Washington's headquarters at the time of the Battle of White Plains. The Purdy house was the finest dwelling in the White Plains area in this period. It was then located on what was known as Dobbs Ferry Road. Here Washington waited for General Howe to move north from New Rochelle. Howe believed that he could engage Washington in one decisive battle, putting a quick end to the war with a British victory. This was not to be, however, and Washington used the Purdy house again in 1778, when the tide of the war had begun to turn in favor of the Americans.

The house has since been moved to its present location on Park Avenue by the Battle of White Plains Monument Committee. Photograph by Renoda Hoffman, Historian of the City of White Plains

Miller House, North White Plains

The Daughters of the American Revolution state that another Washington's headquarters during the Revolution was the Elijah Miller house on Virginia Road, North White Plains. Built in 1738 with an addition in 1770, this is a typical Rhode Island-style farmhouse.

Elijah Miller had fought in the French and Indian War in 1757, where he is said to have become acquainted with Washington. He was an adjutant in the Continental Army when he died in the summer of 1776. His widow and children remained in the house, which Washington is said to have used as a headquarters in October 1776 and again in 1778.

Mrs. Miller nursed sick and wounded soldiers in her home during the war. She also welcomed the organizers of the first Methodist church in White Plains. Francis Asbury preached in the Miller house on his travels throughout Westchester.

The Miller house has been restored by the Washington's Headquarters Chapter of the Daughters of the American Revolution in White Plains. It is open to the public as a museum. Courtesy of Westchester County Historical Society

Thomas Paine was one of the most influential writers of the Revolutionary period. Born in England, he emigrated to the colonies in 1774 and soon became an inspiration to the cause of independence. In 1776 his pamphlet Common Sense *urged permanent separation from England.*

During the war, when discouragement and despair were growing among the Continental troops, Paine issued a series of sixteen pamphlets called The Crisis of the Revolution. *One in 1778 contained the famous exhortation: "These are the times that try men's souls. The summer soldier and the sunshine patriot will, in this crisis, shrink from the service of his country; but he that stands it now, deserves the love and thanks of man and woman." Washington thought these words so moving that he ordered them read in every camp.*

In 1784 the state of New York, in consideration of Paine's wartime services, gave him the confiscated farm of Loyalist Frederick Davoue in New Rochelle. The Thomas Paine cottage, located on North Avenue, is owned and

operated as a museum by the Huguenot-Thomas Paine Historical Association. Courtesy of Westchester County Historical Society

Hanging of Caesar, Irvington

This picture illustrates an episode of a kind all too common in the years of the Neutral Ground. As described in Wolfert's Roost:

> A group of Hessians raided the Odell farm for food...The soldiers seized a Negro slave, Caesar. He refused to tell where the food supply was hidden. They led him to a tree and hanged him. They cut him down. He still refused to tell. Again they hanged him, and cut him down, and again he would not tell. They hanged him a third time and rode off. A family account says that two girls of the household rushed to the rescue. One girl knelt while the other climbed on her back and cut the rope.

Drawing by Lauri Denyer; courtesy of Irvington Historical Society

Feeding and clothing the troops of both American and British armies throughout the entire seven years of the Revolution led to desperate times for all Westchester families. Raiding parties from both sides continually pillaged the countryside, stealing cattle, food, and valuables from Westchester farms and villages. Loyalists who engaged in this thievery were called "Cow Boys," or "Refugees"; patriots stealing from the local people were called "Skinners" since they often stole clothing, "skinning" their victims.

This painting by Charles M. Leffert depicts a group of Loyalists returning from a cattle raid on their old Westchester neighborhoods. The most infamous Cow Boy leader was Colonel James DeLancey, a former high sheriff of Westchester County. *Courtesy of New-York Historical Society, New York*

Ward House, Eastchester

The Ward family of Eastchester provides an example of the divided loyalties that were typical of the Neutral Ground. Stephen Ward was a staunch patriot; his brother Edmund was a Loyalist whose son fought with the British army.

The house shown here is the second Ward house on the same site. The first was built by Stephen Ward in 1730. It was captured by the British during the war and stripped of its siding, which was used to build troop barracks at King's Bridge. The British then burned what was left of the house. The present house, a replica of the first, was built by Stephen Ward's son, Jonathan, after the war. It became a stage stop and post office after the Revolution and now serves as a dormitory for Concordia College. Photograph by Gray Williams, Jr.

Spy Oak, Peekskill

Spies were active on both the British and American sides during 1776 and 1777. British spies tried to help their army recruit troops from among local Loyalists, and American spies tried to stop them. On January 27, 1777, Daniel Strang was hanged from this tree after being convicted of recruiting for the Loyalist Queen's Rangers. The tree, known as the Spy Oak, stands on the grounds of Peekskill High School.

Westchester's most famous patriot spy was Enoch Crosby. He was himself recruited by John Jay and the Committee of Safety to infiltrate Tory circles. Crosby was later immortalized as Harvey Birch in James Fenimore Cooper's novel The Spy. Photograph by Gray Williams, Jr.

THESE are to certify, That *James Richards* entered himfelf a Volunteer in my Company, the *3ᵈ Infant* now in the Battalion of the *Loyal Volunteers* of *New-York,* of which his Excellency Lieutenant-General *James Robertfon,* is Colonel.

New York 4ᵗʰ Auguſt 1781

Blair Templeton Capt.

Approved

A. Weir Lieut: Col:

Loyalist Commission

The British continued to recruit Westchester men to their cause throughout the war. This certificate was issued to James Richards on August 4, 1781, when he joined the Battalion of the Loyal Volunteers of New York. Courtesy of Westchester County Historical Society

Banastre Tarleton

Lieutenant Colonel Banastre Tarleton, Britain's most famous partisan fighter, paid a visit to Pound Ridge on July 3, 1779. His objectives were to attack the militia led by Colonel Elisha Sheldon and to capture Ebenezer Lockwood, an active patriot whose home was Sheldon's headquarters.

Luther Kinnicut, a double agent, walked twenty miles from West Farms (now in the Bronx) to warn Sheldon and Lockwood. Nevertheless, the Americans were caught by surprise when Tarleton attacked at dawn in a fierce rainstorm. Sheldon's troops, greatly outnumbered, retreated, and the British pursued. The militia were encouraged to fight the superior British force by the women along the way who shouted, "Why don't you fight? Why don't you face the enemy? That's good boys! Do something for the good cause! Strike a blow for Congress!" (McDonald Papers).

Tarleton soon gave up the chase and returned to Pound Ridge, where he burned Lockwood's house, the Presbyterian Church, and several other buildings. When the militia turned back to take up the fight, Tarleton and his troops left Pound Ridge and went on to Bedford, where they repeated their burning and plundering. Courtesy of Westchester County Historical Society

In the winter of 1776-1777, Washington left General William Heath in command at Peekskill while he took the main American forces to New Jersey. Command was transferred to General Alexander McDougall in March 1777. Peekskill was an important post with well-stocked storehouses and large barracks, but it was weakly guarded. During the winter it was safe from invasion, but as soon as the ice melted on the Hudson, the British made plans to attack. When General McDougall learned of the British plan, he began to move the precious stores further up the Hudson to Forts Constitution and Montgomery.

The British landed 500 troops at Peekskill on March 22. The American force numbered only 250, so McDougall withdrew, removing as many remaining stores as possible and destroying whatever his troops could not carry. The British then destroyed the barracks and storehouses—a severe loss to the Americans. *Courtesy of Westchester County Historical Society*

British Amphibious Landing at Peekskill

Carpenter House, Valhalla

John André

On February 3, 1780, a large British force attacked Joseph Young's house at Four Corners in Valhalla, because an American force of about 250 men, assigned to guard the line in the area, had stopped nearby. Lieutenant Colonel Joseph Thompson had been ordered to keep on the move to avoid just such a British attack; his failure to obey resulted in disaster. The British killed fourteen Americans and took ninety prisoners.

The Carpenter house was the next target of the British troops. Located near Young's house, it housed several American soldiers who were recovering from smallpox. The British forced all the sick men out into the deep snow, causing their deaths.

The house was formerly located on what is now the Westchester Community College campus. When it was demolished, its eighteenth-century kitchen, shown here in a rare old photograph, was incorporated into the Campbell house, located just across Route 100 from the West Gate of the college. A Campbell ancestor was a Westchester Guide who warned Colonel Thompson that the British were coming but whose warning went unheeded. *Courtesy of Westchester County Historical Society*

Major John André, adjutant general to Sir Henry Clinton, British commander-in-chief, plotted with American General Benedict Arnold to betray the American fortress at West Point in September 1780. Furious at being passed over for promotion and for having been censured for failure to keep adequate financial records, Arnold planned to sell the British information about the fortress, which was considered vital to the American defenses.

André received Clinton's reluctant permission to meet with Arnold for the information. Clinton warned André always to stay in uniform, and not to carry Arnold's secret papers on his person, so he would not be considered a spy if he were captured. It was good advice, but André didn't take it. *Courtesy of Westchester County Historical Society*

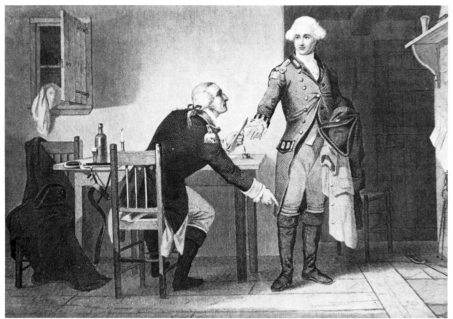

Arnold and Andre Meet

General Clinton sent the British warship *Vulture* up the Hudson to protect André. André used the *Vulture* as a floating head-quarters, but Arnold, fearing detection, refused to meet him there. André was rowed to the western shore on the night of September 20 to meet with the American traitor.

The two men conferred all night by torch-light on the riverbank near Haverstraw. At dawn Arnold suggested that they adjourn to the home of Joshua Hett Smith, his Tory accomplice. While having breakfast, Arnold persuaded André to hide the plans to West Point in his boot. André was soon dismayed to see the *Vulture* sail back down the river, leaving him stranded. *Courtesy of Westchester County Historical Society*

Sparta Cemetery, Ossining

The hole in this tombstone in Sparta Cemetery in Ossining was made by a cannonball fired from the *Vulture* as the British ship returned to New York, leaving André behind enemy lines. On Tellers Point (now Croton Point) the Americans opened fire on the *Vulture*. According to tradition, Jack Peterson, a black militiaman from Peekskill, manned the American cannon as fire was exchanged by both sides.

André was forced to travel overland through Westchester to get back to New York. He disguised himself as a civilian and carried a pass from Arnold stating that he was "John Anderson, on special business." André was now operating not as a British officer, but as a British spy. *Courtesy of Westchester County Historical Society*

Yerkes Tavern, North Salem

On the same morning that André began his journey south through Westchester, a group of Westchester men were making plans at Yerkes Tavern in North Salem. John Yerkes had a permit for a scouting expedition to retrieve cattle stolen by the British, and he asked six young men, all of whom were off duty from the militia, to accompany him. John Paulding, Isaac Van Wart, David Williams, Abraham Williams, Isaac See, and James Romer all agreed, and the group traveled south toward enemy lines.

Yerkes Tavern was demolished in 1932. *Courtesy of Westchester County Historical Society*

Underhill House, Yorktown

Joshua Hett Smith agreed to accompany André into rebel territory, and on September 22 they crossed the Hudson, landing at Verplanck's Point. Carrying Arnold's pass, they successfully talked their way through two American checkpoints between Peekskill and Crompond, where they spent the night. André was so nervous that he wore his boots to bed and did not sleep. At dawn on September 23, they started out once more, stopping for breakfast at the home of Isaac Underhill on Hanover Street in what is now Yorktown Heights. Smith would go no further, so André continued south alone. Photograph by Gray Williams, Jr.

Capture of André at Tarrytown

At Tarrytown the seven young men on their raiding party split into two groups. John Paulding, Isaac Van Wart, and David Williams took up a position in the woods just off the Albany Post Road to watch for passersby, while the others went a little further on. Van Wart was the first to spot André as he approached on horseback. The three young patriots called for him to halt. Paulding was wearing a captured Hessian coat, which made André think the men were Loyalists. He told them he was a British officer, whereupon they informed him that they were Americans. Belatedly, André presented Arnold's pass, but the three made him dismount and take off his boots, good boots being considered very valuable. Inside they discovered the secret papers he was carrying. Paulding was the only one of the three who could read, but all of them realized the importance of what they had discovered. They took André north to Sands' Mill near Armonk, where they turned him over to Lieutenant Colonel John Jameson.

André persuaded Jameson to deliver him up to General Arnold, but Major Benjamin Tallmadge learned of this and convinced Jameson to have André brought back. After spending the night at Colonel Sheldon's headquarters in South Salem, André was taken to West Point. *Courtesy of Westchester County Historical Society*

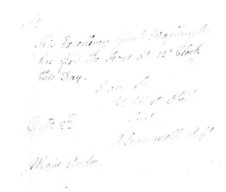

Washington Sets the Time of André's Execution

André remained at West Point until the morning of September 28. He was then transferred to Tappan, where he was tried by court martial and found guilty of spying. André accepted his sentence bravely but wanted to be shot as a soldier rather than to be hanged as a peasant or spy. He wrote to Washington requesting the change, but Washington refused. André had to be hanged, since any change would seem to cast a doubt on his guilt, providing the British with useful propaganda. The brief document shown here set the time of his execution. *Courtesy of Richard Maass, County Historian*

André's Execution

Frantic British efforts were made to save André, and the execution was postponed for one day. The Americans hoped that the British would agree to exchange André for Arnold, but Clinton would not agree.

This nineteenth-century engraving shows André flinching at the sight of the gallows, but in fact, he faced his death without showing fear. At noon on October 2, Colonel Scammell read the death sentence, and André, before placing the rope around his own neck, turned to the large crowd and said, "You all bear witness that I meet my fate as a brave man." Courtesy of Westchester County Historical Society

Van Wart Monument, Elmsford

Van Wart, Paulding, and Williams were greatly honored for their capture of André. The saving of West Point is considered to have been an important factor in America's ultimate victory. Congress awarded each captor a medal and the sum of $200 annually for life. The state of New York gave each a farm valued at $500.

John Paulding lived near Peekskill after the Revolution. He died in 1818 and is buried in St. Peter's Churchyard at Van Cortlandtville. A monument was erected over his grave by the city of New York. Paulding is also represented on the monument erected in Tarrytown near the site of the capture.

David Williams was given a farm in Eastchester but moved with his family in 1805 to Livingstonville, in Schoharie County. He died there in 1831.

Isaac Van Wart lived on a farm in Valhalla. He died in 1828 and is buried in the cemetery of the Dutch Reformed Church in Elmsford. The impressive monument over his grave was erected by the citizens of Westchester County. Courtesy of Westchester County Historical Society

Colonel Christopher Greene

Conditions in Westchester County grew worse in the winter of 1780-1781. Very few American troops were available to protect the local people from the ravages of the British and Loyalists, especially James DeLancey and his Refugees. Colonel Christopher Greene of the First Rhode Island Regiment was placed in command of the lines in northern Westchester. He made his headquarters at the Davenport house in Yorktown. Greene was particularly hated by the British because of his earlier victory over them at Red Bank, New Jersey. Many of his soldiers were black and Indian slaves who had enlisted after a 1778 Rhode Island law permitted slaves to earn their freedom by joining the Continental Army. Courtesy of Westchester County Historical Society

Davenport House, Yorktown

DeLancey and 300 Refugees rode thirty miles north from Morrisania on May 12, 1781. They passed all the American patrols in the area without detection, but only 200 were able to ford the swollen Croton River to get to their target, the Davenport house and Colonel Greene. It was just about dawn on May 13 when the attack began. Greene, Major Ebenezer Flagg, and a young lieutenant were asleep in a second-floor bedroom. About fifty American troops were in

tents scattered around the house, but the savage attack came so quickly that the Americans had no time to prepare. In a few minutes Greene was mortally wounded, his officers and six other soldiers killed, and thirty-three men taken prisoner.

Taking Greene with them, the Refugees then headed down the road for the Griffen house, where most of Greene's Rhode Island troops were quartered. The Refugees left Greene near death by the side of the road and went up to the

house, announcing that Colonel Greene was dead and demanding that the Americans surrender. The former slaves fought bravely but were all killed.

The Davenport house, located on Croton Heights Road, was owned for several years by the Westchester County Historical Society. It is now a private residence. Photograph by Renoda Hoffman; courtesy of Westchester County Historical Society

America sought the help of the French throughout the Revolution. France at first responded by contributing money to the American cause, but at length, the French were persuaded to send troops as well. On July 12, 1780, 5,000 French soldiers landed at Newport, Rhode Island. Their commander was General Jean-Baptiste Donatien de Vimeur, Comte de Rochambeau, shown here in a sketch by John Trumbull done for his painting, Surrender of Cornwallis.

The French army at Newport remained inactive the better part of a year. In early July 1781 Rochambeau and his troops finally marched south through Connecticut and into Westchester to meet Washington and his army. Washington planned to attack the British stronghold in New York City, but Rochambeau convinced him that this would be unwise because the Americans did not have a supporting fleet in New York Harbor. Courtesy of Westchester County Historical Society

For six weeks, from July 6 until August 18, 1781, Rochambeau occupied the house of John Odell on Ridge Road in Hartsdale. During this time he and Washington, who was using the nearby Appleby house as his headquarters, awaited word from Admiral de Grasse and the French navy. Finally de Grasse informed them that his ships would be off the Virginia coast and could support any action in that region. Washington and Rochambeau quickly decided to move on to Yorktown, Virginia, to do battle with Cornwallis. Rochambeau gave Washing-

ton $20,000 with which to pay the American troops so they would make the long march south. The American success at the Battle of Yorktown resulted in the articles of capitulation signed October 19, 1781.

John Odell was a famous Westchester Guide. His descendants lived in the farmhouse in Hartsdale until 1965. It was then deeded by the family to the New York chapter of the Sons of the Revolution to be restored and maintained. Photograph from Sanchis, American Architecture: Westchester County

The period from 1783, when the war ended, until 1787, when the Constitution was adopted, was one of transition in Westchester County. During this time, Westchester was divided into two shires, and Bedford and White Plains were selected as the sites of Westchester's two courthouses. In 1786, £1,800 was appropriated for the building of courthouses and jails in both towns since most public buildings in each had been destroyed during the war.

The Bedford Court House, located on the northern point of the triangular Bedford Green, appears today much as it must have looked in 1787. This picture, depicting the public reading of the Constitution to the new United States citizens of Bedford, is a mural in the Manhattan Savings Bank in Mount Kisco. Courtesy of Westchester County Historical Society

Reading the Constitution at the Bedford Court House

49

Chapter 2

1783-1865:
The Pastoral Life

The Revolution devastated Westchester County. Seven years of raids and plundering left much of the countryside a waste. Many homes had been burned. The population of the county was reduced by more than 1,000 through war casualties and the emigration of Loyalists to Canada and England. The former Loyalists who remained were often the objects of bitter resentment. In 1784 Bedford citizens voted at a town meeting that "no persons that have been over to the Enemy shall come to the town to reside. And if any have already come in, they are to be immediately Drove out" (Griffin, *Westchester County and Its People*).

As Westchester began the task of rebuilding, there was one big change that benefited local farmers. Many of the landholdings in the county had belonged to Loyalists and were confiscated by the state and sold by the Commissioners of Forfeiture. In all, the Westchester holdings of fifty-four Loyalists were thus sold off; the largest of these was Philipsburgh Manor. As a result of such sales, many farmers were able to buy the lands they had previously farmed as tenants.

In 1788 the county was formally divided into twenty towns. The first federal census, taken in 1790, showed a Westchester population of 24,000, mostly concentrated in the northern part. The chief occupation was farming, and during the early part of the nineteenth century, subsistence farming was the rule. Crops included potatoes and other vegetables, fruit, corn, and wheat. Every farm had dairy cows and poultry, and sheep were grazed on land too rough for cultivation.

As New York City recovered from British occupation, Westchester farmers began to sell their cattle and produce there. Sing Sing (now Ossining), on the Hudson, and Sawpit (now Port Chester), on the Sound, were the main ports to which farmers delivered their crops for shipment to New York. Cattle were driven directly to city markets on the hoof.

Improved roads were a necessity for getting both cattle and crops to market. In 1800 the first commercial toll road, the Westchester Turnpike, was chartered, running through Pelham and New Rochelle. Toll gates were erected at intervals, and the charge was four cents for a horse and rider, ten cents for a one-horse passenger vehicle, and twenty cents for a stagecoach. In the northern part of the county, the Croton Turnpike (also called the Somerstown Turnpike) linked Somers to the Hudson River at Sing Sing. The turnpikes were made free public roads by the middle of the nineteenth century.

In addition to the turnpikes, the Albany, Danbury, and Boston post roads were used to convey produce to market, as well as to carry the mail. These roads were also the main routes for stagecoach travel. Taverns and inns did a brisk business along these main roads. Taverns also often served as post offices. For example, the Ward house in Eastchester (seen in chapter I) was both tavern and post office after the Revolution.

Despite the gradual improvement of the roads, travel by water remained the most practical and convenient way to get both passengers and freight to New York. Sloops made regular stops at the docks of the towns along the Hudson. Steamboats began to ply the river after Robert Fulton's *Clermont* made its first Hudson trip in 1807. The steamboats, however, landed on the west side of the Hudson; Westchester passengers had to be rowed out to board them. Sloops and steamboats shared the water transport business for many years on both the Hudson and the Sound.

Ede Mennona Works the Loom at Van Cortlandt Manor
Courtesy of Sleepy Hollow Restorations

As the economy of the new nation began to expand, small industries developed in Westchester. Cottage industries, chiefly shoemaking, had been prevalent before the Revolution, providing farming families with a small but welcome cash income. After the war these occupations began to be carried on in "factories." The work was still largely done by hand, but in buildings, often barns, specifically devoted to that purpose.

Only gradually were larger industries established. Iron foundries in Port Chester, Peekskill, and Morrisania (now part of the Bronx) made stoves and plowshares. Brickyards grew up in Croton and Verplanck. Marble quarries in Tuckahoe, Sing Sing, Hastings, and Thornwood supplied the nation with the building material necessary for the neoclassic architecture so popular in the nation's public buildings. For instance, many federal buildings destroyed by the British during the War of 1812 were rebuilt with Westchester marble. The local marble quarries were the main reason that New York State chose Sing Sing as the site of a new prison, begun in 1825.

Two developments in the 1830s and 1840s had an enormous effect on Westchester's growth. The first was the construction of the Croton Dam and Aqueduct, and the second was the building of the railroads. New York City's importance in the history of Westchester County is nowhere more apparent than in the watershed construction that began in the 1830s. The Croton River was determined to be the best source of water for the rapidly growing metropolis, and despite the misgivings of many local residents, the first Croton Dam was begun in 1837 and completed in 1842.

The railroads came in the 1840s. By the summer of 1842, the New York and Harlem Railroad was running trains as far as Williamsbridge, and by 1844 the railroad had reached White Plains. The New York and Hudson River Railroad was being constructed in the same period and reached Peekskill in 1849. On the east side of the county, the New York, New Haven and Hartford opened its line in 1849. Both the railroads and the New York City water system were constructed chiefly by Irish laborers, who were emigrating in large numbers during this period to escape the famine in their native land.

One of the effects of rail service in Westchester was the shift from subsistence farming to dairying. Many farms began producing milk commercially once the railroads were available to make daily "milk runs."

The coming of the railroads brought a shift in population from

One Room School, Bedford
Photograph by Gray Williams, Jr.

the northern part of the county to the southern. Before the railroads, the most populous town in Westchester was Bedford. Between 1845 and 1855, the population of the county increased by 33,000, with most of the people choosing to live in the towns close to the railroad lines. The area of Eastchester that became Mount Vernon was hardly settled at all before 1850. In that year John Stevens of New York organized the Industrial Home Association No. 1, bought 367 acres of farmland in Eastchester, and laid out streets and building lots for a new town. This type of development was to be repeated in other sections of Westchester. By 1860 the total population of the county was 99,000, and Yonkers was the largest city.

Social life in Westchester during the first half of the nineteenth century revolved very much around church, school, and home. While churches after the Revolution were no longer involved in politics, they remained centers of community life. New churches were built and old ones rebuilt. Evangelical meetings like the Methodist Camp Meeting, established in 1834 at Sing Sing, were enormously popular.

Public schools were first established in Westchester County through an act of the New York legislature in 1795. A later act, in 1812, established the State Superintendent of Common Schools, thus creating the first state system of education in the country. Westchester's public schools in the nineteenth century were generally small, one-room affairs, but private schools also began to flourish early in the century. Notable examples were the North Salem and Bedford academies, and the Mount Pleasant Military Academy in Ossining.

While most Westchester citizens were hard-working farmers and small businessmen, there was a scattering of wealthy and nationally-known residents. John Jay and his descendants lived in Katonah. Washington Irving built Sunnyside on the Hudson River at Tarrytown. Artists such as Robert Havell, Jr., chose the Hudson River area for their homes and shared its beauty with the world through their paintings.

The Civil War had a great effect on Westchester even though fighting never touched county soil. At the outbreak of the war, many residents had mixed feelings about the strong anti-slavery stand of Lincoln and the Republicans. Lincoln did not carry the county in 1860 or 1864.

After the Southern states seceded, however, sentiment shifted toward solid support for the Union. Many young Westchester men volunteered. Once the initial enthusiasm wore off and there were fewer volunteers, towns began to offer bounties to entice men to sign up. This system was not successful, however, so in March 1863 a draft law was enacted. Draft rioters in New York moved up into Westchester but were persuaded to disband.

Throughout the war, Westchester citizens contributed what they could to the war effort. Church bells rang out in every town for each Union victory, and people gathered in the churches for public readings of the few available newspapers. Ladies' groups sewed clothing and made bandages to send to the soldiers in the field.

The end of the war brought problems created by the readjustment of returning soldiers, a greatly increased cost of living, and a slower growth in population. The more industrial southern part of Westchester grew faster than ever, however, and the county was soon ready to begin a new era of prosperity. ■

Fitch Homestead, Lewisboro

The Fitch homestead, in the Vista section of the town of Lewisboro, is typical of the simple dwellings of the farm families who re-established the rural life of Westchester County in the years following the Revolution. This picture was taken in the early 1900s, when the house probably still looked much as it had a century before. Notice the wellsweep on the left side of the picture. It was once a common piece of farmyard equipment, designed to lift a full bucket of water by its counterweight. The bucket had to be relatively small and the sweep very long.

The Fitch house is gone today, but others similar to it remain in Vista. Photograph by Charles Bouton; courtesy of Doris Bouton Tether

Cudner-Hyatt House, Scarsdale

The Cudner-Hyatt house is one of the few remaining farmhouses in Scarsdale. The north end of the house was built about 1735 by Mikiah Cudner, a tenant farmer on Scarsdale Manor. Its subsequent history is typical of old Westchester farmhouses. In 1836 the property was purchased by Caleb Hyatt, who enlarged the house by doubling the floor plan and raising the loft to a full second story. A separate structure, probably a barn, was moved up and attached to the house. The farm was broken up in the late nineteenth century, but the house remained in the Hyatt family until 1972. It is now owned by the Scarsdale Historical Society, which is carrying out its interior restoration. Courtesy of Scarsdale Historical Society

Alfred Mead House, Waccabuc

This photograph, taken early in this century, recalls rural Westchester life of an earlier period. Alice Mead Neergaard, wearing her grandmother's dress, sits among the antique furnishings of the Alfred Mead house. Alfred Mead built his homestead in 1820, on Mead Street in Waccabuc. The family settled in Waccabuc, a hamlet of the town of Lewisboro, before the Revolution, and many members of the family still live there. The Mead house itself is now occupied by relatives of the family. Courtesy of Westchester County Historical Society

Team of Oxen, Harrison

The economy of early Westchester was agricultural, but the agriculture practiced here was very different from that of Europe. Maize, for example, which formed a substantial part of the diet of people and animals, was strictly a New World product. The early settlers had to learn from the Indians how to grow it and prepare it for food. There were few horses on the farms, and teams of oxen performed most of the heavy animal labor. Courtesy of Charles Dawson History Center, Harrison

Haying, Pound Ridge

This picture shows a scene common on Westchester farms throughout the nineteenth century. Here, Clay Brown and Sam Varian are haying in Weed Meadow on Barnegat Road in Pound Ridge. Courtesy of Pound Ridge Historical Society

Shad Fishing on the Hudson River

The Hudson River has always been a productive fishing ground, as noted by Henry Hudson in his journal when he first explored the river. During the nineteenth century, many Westchester farmers would leave their land for several weeks each spring to camp on the river banks and fish for shad and striped bass during the spawning run. The catch, salted down, became an important staple during the rest of the year. Courtesy of Hudson River Museum, Yonkers

Square House, Rye

Milestone, White Plains

The building of good roads was of primary importance to the development of Westchester. The first post roads in America were established in 1753 by Deputy Postmaster General Benjamin Franklin. Franklin devised the use of milestones along these roads; in Westchester they show the distance to New York City Hall. Because the roads have been changed somewhat over the years, the recorded distances are no longer exactly correct.

Most of the remaining milestones in Westchester are probably nineteenth-century replacements for the original pre-Revolutionary stones. The milestone shown here, however, dates from before the war. It was originally located on Maple Avenue (formerly the Post Road) in White Plains. It was moved to the site of the Armory in 1932 in order to preserve it and in 1981 was placed in the White Plains Public Library. *Courtesy of White Plains Public Library/Renoda Hoffman*

Travel over the early roads was slow and often arduous and required frequent stops to change the horses. The old Boston Post Road, going back to before the Revolution, had many taverns and inns to offer the travel-weary shelter and food. One of the most famous was the Square House at the end of Purchase Street in Rye, which was built as a private home around 1730. The Reverend James Wetmore was the first to use the building as a tavern; his son Timothy was tavern keeper. In the days preceding the Revolution, taverns were not just drinking houses, but centers of community life, and a tavern keeper had to be approved by the city fathers.

In 1770 Dr. Ebenezer Haviland and his wife purchased the Square House, and it was during their ownership that the tavern became famous. Illustrious guests included John Adams in 1774 and George Washington in 1789. Washington wrote that the Widow Haviland (her husband had been killed serving as a surgeon in the Continental Army) "keeps a very neat and decent inn."

From 1801 until 1830 the tavern was operated by Nathaniel Penfield. It then became a private residence until 1903, when it was taken over for the town hall of the newly-formed village of Rye. In 1964 a new municipal building was completed, and the Square House was leased to the Rye Historical Society, which restored it and now operates it as a museum. *Photograph from Sanchis, American Architecture: Westchester County*

Smith's Tavern, Armonk

Smith's Tavern, on Bedford Road in Armonk, is believed to have been built in the late 1700s. John Smith, a former captain in the Continental Army, operated the house as a tavern, post office, and stopping place for the Danbury stage as early as 1797. Smith was active in town politics, and his tavern was a major local meeting place. Smith's son Samuel continued to operate the tavern until his own death in 1884. Since 1974 the building has belonged to the North Castle Historical Society and is now open to the public as a museum. Photograph by Gray Williams, Jr.

Albany Stage

Easy access to New York City by water tended to delay the development of good roads. Nevertheless, weekly stages were established by 1784 between New York and Albany along the Albany Post Road, now Route 9. The Albany stage was only halted when the railroad superseded it around the middle of the nineteenth century. The stagecoaches could carry twenty passengers, and in winter the wheeled coaches were replaced with sleighs. The stages made frequent stops at inns and taverns along the way, allowing passengers to rest and eat, and delivering mail and New York City newspapers to the local townspeople.

Central Westchester was also served by stagecoach lines. The Danbury stage, for example, came through Lewisboro, Bedford, and White Plains before connecting at Tarrytown with steamboats bound for New York. *Courtesy of Huguenot-Thomas Paine Historical Association, New Rochelle*

Van Cortlandt Ferry House, Croton

Bridges were constructed over narrow streams to connect the roads on either side, but the wider rivers required ferries. The ferries, in turn, necessitated ferry houses. The ferry house near Van Cortlandt Manor House in Croton provided refreshments and lodging for travelers crossing the Croton River on the Albany Post Road. The ferry had been established in the eighteenth century, when Philip Van Cortlandt owned Van Cortlandt Manor. It was designed to meet the needs of increased traffic along the road, then called Queen's Highway. Operation of the ferry was entrusted to one of the manor tenants. *Courtesy of Sleepy Hollow Restorations*

By the time John D. Rockefeller, Jr., bought the Van Cortlandt Manor House to have it restored and preserved, the ferry house and its kitchen buildings had been demolished. The present buildings, part of Van Cortlandt Manor operated by Sleepy Hollow Restorations, are a reconstruction. *Courtesy of Sleepy Hollow Restorations*

Van Cortlandt Ferry House, Croton

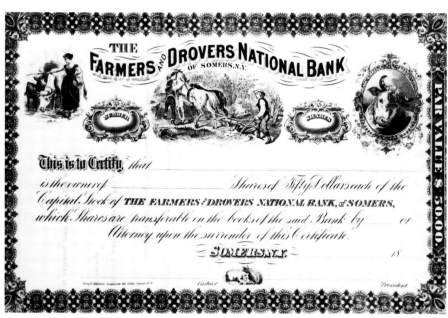

Farmers and Drovers Bank Certificate, Somers

Somers was a major population center during the first half of the nineteenth century. It was the eastern terminus of the Croton Turnpike, the main route for northern Westchester farmers taking their cattle and produce to Sing Sing for shipment to New York. Local commerce produced the need for a bank, and in 1839 the Farmers and Drovers Bank was organized. The illustrations seen in this copy of the bank's stock certificate point up the agricultural economy of northern Westchester.

The bank's first president was Horace Bailey, cousin of the circus entrepreneur Hachaliah Bailey. The bank was housed at Somers in the Elephant Hotel and in the small wooden building adjacent to it. In 1896 the Farmers and Drovers Bank was absorbed by the Mount Kisco National Bank. *Courtesy of Somers Historical Society*

Croton Turnpike Toll Scrip

Commercial turnpikes were necessary to the prosperity of the county's interior as they permitted access to the waterways on either side of the county. The chief market for the agricultural products of Westchester was New York, and the best way to get there was by boat. The Croton Turnpike was incorporated in 1807 for the purpose of building a road from Somers to Sing Sing (now Ossining). The scrip pictured here was used by turnpike travelers to pay the tolls. The road's operators received most of the tolls for cattle being driven to market. The Croton Turnpike remained in operation until 1849, when it became a free road. *Courtesy of Westchester County Historical Society*

Van Cortlandt Ferry House Tap Room

The tap room of the Van Cortlandt Manor ferry house, shown here as reconstructed by Sleepy Hollow Restorations, must have been a welcome spot for tired travelers along the Albany Post Road. A good hot meal and a hearty drink from one of the tankards on the table, plus the conviviality of the ferry house guests, offered a chance to revive spirits weary from the long trip between New York and Albany. *Courtesy of Sleepy Hollow Restorations*

Sing Sing Village

This view, overlooking the village of Sing Sing, which indicates the importance of the village as a port on the busy Hudson River, was executed by W. H. Bartlett. In the nineteenth century, Sing Sing was the center to which farmers from the northern part of the county brought their produce and livestock, either to be sold in Market Square or to be shipped by sloop and steamboat to New York City.

This village area of the town of Mount Pleasant grew so populous that in 1845 a new township was created. Sing Sing and Sparta, its neighbor hamlet to the south, are today part of the town of Ossining. Courtesy of Westchester County Historical Society

61

Captain King's Sloop *Eliza Ann*, Dobb Ferry

Shipping continued to be the most efficient means of transporting goods and people. Sloops were a common sight on the Hudson and the Sound. One of the most successful of the river captains was John King, who came to Dobbs Ferry in 1821. He learned of the demand in New York City for pickle-size cucumbers and began to concentrate on cucumber growing at his farm on Willow Point (near the present Dobbs Ferry railroad station).

King's sloop Eliza Ann (named for his wife, the former Eliza Ann Dobbs) sailed three times a week from Dobbs Ferry to New York. In good weather the trip took two hours, but headwinds and an adverse tide could extend the time to five. Hudson River sloop owners like Captain King had a near monopoly on transporting both goods and people to and from the city. Captains also acted as commission agents, selling produce for local farmers and purchasing tools and other goods for them in New York.

King retired from the Hudson River in 1841 and moved to Ardsley, where he operated his King Pickle Works factory for many years. Photograph from Life of a River Village: Dobbs Ferry

Henry Clay Fire, Hudson River

The steamboat revolutionized transportation and commerce with its increased speed and independence of wind power and tides. But it was not without its own particular perils, as this picture clearly indicates. July 28, 1852, has been called "the Hudson's blackest day." On this date the steamboat Henry Clay, carrying between 300 and 400 passengers, caught fire. Although the passengers who boarded at Albany that morning thought they were on a routine trip to New York City, the Henry Clay was in fact racing another ship, the Armenia. Both ships had been built by Thomas Collyer of Sing Sing, and he was still the principal owner of the Henry Clay. The two ships were neck and neck for most of the journey. Scheduled stops were passed right by as each captain called for more steam in his attempt to get to New York first.

The Henry Clay was slightly ahead at 2:45 p.m. as she came past Yonkers. Suddenly there was the shout "Fire!" as smoke billowed from the overheated boilers. The ship went aground at the bow, but most of the passengers were trapped on the stern, which was in deep water. Sixty people died, including the sister of Nathaniel Hawthorne and the noted architect Andrew Jackson Downing.

The owners of the Henry Clay were later tried for manslaughter but acquitted. A monument to eight unidentified victims was erected in St. John's Cemetery in Yonkers. Courtesy of Hudson River Museum, Yonkers

Old Mill, Harrison

Hunt's General Store, Cross River

During the nineteenth century, general stores were the shopping centers in Westchester communities and had to satisfy virtually all needs for goods from outside the community. John Hunt, who operated this store in Cross River, sold everything from meat to yard goods and served as postmaster of Cross River as well.

When the New Croton Dam was constructed between 1892 and 1905, the town of Cross River was cut in two, and Hunt's store, located on the Danbury Post Road, was torn down. *Courtesy of Westchester County Historical Society*

While Westchester was mainly rural until after the Civil War, industry played an increasingly significant role in county life. The earliest industries were mills—the sawmills and grist-mills that were built on the rivers that supplied their power. The mill at the Old Mill Farm on West Street in Harrison is one of the few early mill buildings in Westchester to survive today.

An Indian legend associated with the property tells of a great white deer's yearly visit to the nearby falls in the river. An Indian lucky enough to see the deer would have good fortune and success for an entire year.

John Richbell is said to have bought the property from the Indians. He sold it to a Mr. Griffen, who built the mill, perhaps as early as 1720. The mill had several owners over the years and was operated commercially until 1925. Note that the mill wheel is overshot, with the water flowing over the top of the wheel to turn it. This is an advancement over the undershot wheel of the eighteenth-century mills like Philipsburgh Manor Upper Mills. *Courtesy of Westchester County Historical Society*

Dougherty's Horse and Ox Shoeing, Harrison

Like milling of grain and corn, smithing was another craft essential to every community. James Dougherty ran this blacksmith shop, located across from Macy Street and Halsted Avenue (current site of the Harrison Shopping Center) in Harrison, until around 1915. Throughout the nineteenth century, local farmers continued to depend upon oxen as their principal draft animals, and Mr. Dougherty shod oxen as well as horses. Such village blacksmiths played another important role in Westchester rural life as well; they mended the tools and other equipment necessary to the farmer's work.

Mr. Dougherty also served as blacksmith to the wealthy people who began to move into the area around the end of the century, and who came to him to have their fine horses shod and their fancy carriages repaired. Courtesy of Charles Dawson History Center, Harrison

Cobbler's Bench, Pound Ridge

Shoemaking was a widespread cottage industry in the early 1800s throughout rural Westchester for it enabled farm families to make a small cash income and kept them busy during the winter months. Nowhere was this craft more prevalent than in Pound Ridge, where almost 150 families were shoemakers. Pre-cut shoe parts were obtained from New Canaan and Long Ridge, Connecticut. Women and children did the fine stitching of the uppers, and the men fit the uppers over the last and attached the soles. The shoes were made to fit either foot and in the 1820s cost $1.20 a pair. A family could earn seven to fifteen dollars per week, depending on speed and skill.

Cobblers of the Scofield family were famous for their Lancaster clogs, pictured here on a cobbler's bench still owned by the family. In making these clogs, with their wooden soles and stitched uppers, the Scofields used techniques handed down from their ancestors in Lancaster, England. Photograph by Susan Swanson

Charles Scofield's Shoe Factory, Pound Ridge

Shoemaking as a home industry died out in the middle of the century when power-operated machinery was developed for use in factories. Early shoe factories, such as Charles Scofield's, were in reality barns or sheds. Scofield's factory was located on Route 124 across from the James Delihas house. It was taken down in the 1930s. Courtesy of Pound Ridge Historical Society

Ice Cutting on Crystal Lake, New Rochelle

The cutting of ice on local ponds and lakes was a widespread winter activity throughout rural Westchester. On Crystal Lake in New Rochelle it became a thriving industry. Large icehouses were built in the 1840s, and a conveyor was constructed to transport the ice over Main Street. Paddlewheel steamers carried the ice to New York City. From the 1840s to the 1860s Crystal Lake was the main source of the ice for New York and Brooklyn markets.

The ice business waned during the Civil War, and the lake became stagnant and a breeding ground for mosquitoes. After the war, John Stephenson purchased the lake and had it drained. In the early 1900s the site became the Stephenson Park residential area. Courtesy of Huguenot-Thomas Paine Historical Association, New Rochelle

The Old Stone Mill, built between 1800 and 1810 on the Bronx River in Tuckahoe, was one of the first cotton mills in the United States. There was once a large bell on top of the building, used to call the local people to work. The mill was a welcome addition to the economy of the area as it gave local farm families an opportunity to earn ready money. The mill was operated until 1821 and then stood vacant until 1853, when it became part of the Hodgman Rubber Company. After Hodgman moved to Massachusetts in 1925, the mill was acquired by the Burroughs-Wellcome drug firm. Today Burroughs-Wellcome is the U.S.V. Pharmaceutical Company, and the Old Stone Mill houses its engineering department. Courtesy of Westchester County Historical Society

Old Stone Mill, Tuckahoe

Underhill Brickyard, Croton

A brick industry flourished from Croton to Verplanck from the 1840s. It continued until the lack of clay and the increased use of other building materials caused it to die out in the early twentieth century. By the 1850s there were thirty-seven plants operating in the town of Cortlandt, employing over 1,000 people.

William Underhill's brickyard on Croton Point began operating in 1837, and every brick manufactured there was marked with his initials. Note that the roofs and walls of the buildings can be opened to facilitate drying the bricks. A small community, complete with school, store, tavern, and boardinghouse for seasonal workers, grew up around the brickyard. The family operated the business until 1880, and the Underhill Brick Company continued in existence until 1915. Courtesy of Historical Reference Room, Croton Public Library

65

Marble Quarry, Tuckahoe

Marble outcroppings in Westchester County, chiefly in Tuckahoe, have been worked commercially since the early 1800s. Alexander Masterton's ownership of the Tuckahoe quarry brought the industry its most prosperous period. He employed many Irish stonecutters who had fled the famines of the 1830s and 1840s. Italian workers came to join the Irish working the quarries in the 1890s.

The neoclassic style so prevalent in nineteenth-century architecture assured a market for marble, especially in public buildings. Masterton won a contract to repair and rebuild the public buildings in Washington, D. C., that had been damaged during the War of 1812. The Washington Monument and the Capitol, as well as major buildings in other cities all over the United States, were built with marble from the Tuckahoe quarry. There were other marble quarries as well, located at Hastings, Sing Sing, and Thornwood.

In the early days, teams of oxen pulled marble to the docks in drays. But the quarry owners were among the first to see the advantages of the new railroad being discussed in the 1840s. Tradition says that they raised $15,000 to help bring the railroad north from New York; in any event, Tuckahoe was for some time the only regular stop between the Bronx and White Plains.

The marble industry in Westchester largely died out in the early 1900s. Improved transportation made higher quality marble from Tennessee and Vermont more available throughout the country. Also, changing architectural fashions decreased the demand. Courtesy of Westchester County Historical Society

Sing Sing Prison, Ossining

In April 1825 New York State prison officials picked Mount Pleasant (now Ossining) as the site of a new prison. The village was chosen mainly because local stone quarries offered profitable labor for the prisoners. Its location, directly on the Hudson River, also facilitated the transport of quarried stone and other products made by the prisoners. One hundred convicts were brought from the state prison at Auburn to build the new facility, which was completed in October 1828.

The prison was originally named the Mount Pleasant State Prison, but was later renamed Sing Sing Prison, when the town adopted Sing Sing as its new name in 1845. Anti-prison feeling in the town developed, however, and the town changed its name again, to Ossining, in 1901. Today Sing Sing Prison has changed its name to the Ossining Correctional Facility, but to most local people it will always be known as "Sing Sing."

The lockstep and striped uniforms, shown here, were abolished in the 1890s. Courtesy of Ossining Historical Society

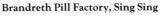

Brandreth Pill Factory, Sing Sing

During the first half of the nineteenth century, there were a few major manufacturing enterprises in the county. Brandreth Pill Factory was one of the most successful.

Benjamin Brandreth was born in England in 1809. He was the grandson of a doctor who had devised the formula for a successful patent medicine in 1751. Brandreth entered the family medicine business at an early age, and by 1828 he was buying out the company interests of other family members.

Effective advertising made Brandreth pills a success in America as well as in England, and in 1835 Brandreth moved to New York. He believed that all diseases were caused by impurities in the blood and that his purgative pills would remove the impurities and effect a cure.

In 1837 Brandreth moved to Sing Sing, where his Brandreth Pill Factory produced pills by the millions. Seen here are factory workers filling the small, oval pillboxes. Brandreth built a thirty-room mansion, married Virginia Graham of Sing Sing, and had twelve children. He was active in both local and state politics. When Westchester boys left home in 1861 to fight in the Civil War, Brandreth gave each of them a supply of Brandreth pills.

Brandreth died in 1880, and his children carried on his business for forty-seven years. The factory buildings on Water Street in Ossining are now occupied by the Filex Corporation. Courtesy of Ossining Historical Society

Brandreth Advertising Poster

In 1848 Brandreth bought an interest in Allcocks Porous Plasters and along with Thomas Allcock organized the firm of Thomas Allcock and Company.

While Brandreth's advertising relied heavily on the testimonials of satisfied customers, posters such as this one were also in vogue. Brightly colored to catch the eye, these posters must have helped to make Brandreth a household name. Courtesy of Ossining Historical Society

67

Westchester County Savings Bank, Tarrytown

By mid-century, Westchester towns had developed sufficient population to support banking institutions for the personal needs of the citizenry as well as for commercial interests. The Westchester County Savings Bank was organized by a group of fourteen men who met at the Franklin House (later known as Florence Inn) in Tarrytown on August 2, 1853. Savings banks were a relatively new concept in America; the first had been established in Boston only thirty-seven years before. Among the incorporators of the new bank were members of old local families and several New York businessmen who lived in Tarrytown. They included Washington Irving and James Watson Webb, editor of the New York Courier and Inquirer.

In 1864 the bank moved from rented space to its own building, a house bought from Stephen York at the main intersection of town—Turnpike Road (now Broadway) and Main Street. In 1898 the frame house was replaced by a yellow brick building in Spanish Renaissance style. This building, expanded and modernized in 1933, remains the home of the bank today. The Westchester County Savings Bank has merged with several other savings banks in the county to become Peoples Westchester Savings Bank. Courtesy of Peoples Westchester Savings Bank

View of North Salem

By 1820 an era of growth began in Westchester with improvement of roads, the growth of some industry, and an increasing population, all of which led to the development of thriving villages.

These were peak days for North Salem, which was to begin to decline in the 1880s. By the 1850s there were mills for grinding corn, oats, and wheat, and for pressing apples into cider and vinegar. There were sawmills, a paper mill, and factories for making carriages, woolens, shirts and hats, and the handles of farm implements. Main Street was lined with shops of all kinds, and there were several hotels for visitors to the Peach Lake resort area. Courtesy of North Salem Historical Society

The Croton Dam, built between 1837 and 1842, changed the geography of Westchester and also its population. More than 1,300 people, laborers and their families, immigrated into the county, seeking employment on the enormous project. When the dam was completed, most of the newcomers, largely Irish, stayed in Westchester, finding work in the building industry, brickyards, and on the railroads.

In early January 1841, when the dam was nearly completed, an eighteen-inch snow storm, followed by three days of rain, caused the Croton River to rise so high that it broke the dam. Fortunately, dam officials had time enough to dispatch messengers to warn people downstream. The flood swept away houses, mills, and bridges along the entire course of the river and left so much silt that the mouth of the Croton River was closed to shipping forever.

Only a few lives were lost because of the early warning.

The dam was rebuilt, this time entirely of masonry rather than the combination of masonry and earthwork that had proved too weak. The dam is still intact but is now submerged under the New Croton Reservoir and becomes visible only in periods of severe drought. *Courtesy of Westchester County Historical Society*

69

Croton Aqueduct Double Arch, Ossining

The Croton Dam backed up the Croton River for five miles and created a reservoir of about 400 acres. To carry the water to New York, an aqueduct was built, connecting to a receiving reservoir at Fifth Avenue and Forty-second Street, the present site of Bryant Park behind the New York Public Library.

In some parts of the county, the aqueduct tunnels below the gorund; in other places, it crosses gorges through arched viaducts. The most spectacular example of this is the double arch at Ossining, where an eighty-eight-foot stone arch spans the Kill Brook. In the 1860s, a second arch was constructed, under the aqueduct arch, to carry the traffic of Broadway across the brook. A promenade with a protective railing was added to the top of the aqueduct arch. The double arch is still in Ossining but is now difficult to see because of subsequent overgrowth. Courtesy of Ossining Historical Society

The Croton Maid

When the Croton Aqueduct was completed, in 1842, a final inspection was conducted by members of the New York City Board of Water Commissioners before water was let through. The thirty-three-mile walk, by lantern light, took two days.

Two weeks later, when the first few inches of water had been let into the tunnel, a few brave souls floated down the dark aqueduct on a flat-bottomed boat they christened the Croton Maid.

Once a year the aqueduct was drained and inspected for cracks. For the four to five days this procedure took, New York City had to rely on the water in the Central Park Reservoir. By 1869 this temporary water supply was no longer adequate, so from then on, repairs were made only in cases of extreme necessity. Drawing by Lauri Denyer; courtesy of Irvington Historical Society

Croton Aqueduct at Yonkers

The most visible sections of the Croton Aqueduct are the stone embankments built to carry the aqueduct conduit over existing streams or roads. These stone embankments are covered with a protective layer of dirt. In Yonkers, the embankment carries the aqueduct over Nepperhan Avenue. Courtesy of Huguenot-Thomas Paine Historical Association, New Rochelle

Hudson River Railroad Locomotive

The railroads, built during the 1840s, were to create a new Westchester, for with them came the feasibility of commuting to New York. As quickly as the railroad lines were in place, New Yorkers began to move out of the city to live in the rural beauty of Westchester.

The Hudson River Railroad reached Peekskill by 1849 with five trains running daily from New York. Construction of the railroad had been opposed by the steamship lines, but ice on the Hudson River, which halted the steamers during the winter months, gave the needed impetus to the railroad builders. The coming of the railroad heralded the end of the steamship era, although both modes of transportation operated side-by-side for many years. The opening of the railroad was announced in a local newspaper as follows:

> New York to Peekskill—42 miles in 59 minutes. The Road is now fully tested, and found to be in prime running order; and daily the iron horse whirs to and fro along the track between these points, and causing the vallies to re-echo with his shrill whistle for miles along his path. The cars to be placed upon this Road, are of the most superb finish and comfort, and the engines are of unsurpassed speed and power; and everything in connection with it tends to render it superior in fitness and facility of travel to any road in the country, and we doubt not the patronage of the Road will be immense (Hufeland Scrapbooks).

Courtesy of Westchester County Historical Society

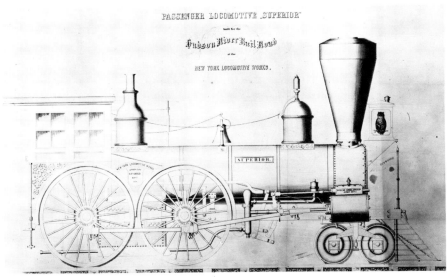

Railroad—Stage Connection, North Castle to Port Chester

When the railroads came to Westchester, stages began the service of meeting trains and carrying passengers to and from the stations, much as taxis meet commuter trains today.

Hiram Finch advertised his stage line in 1850, as shown here. The trip took three hours each way and cost 37½¢. If passengers were willing to pay extra, Mr. Finch would go off his regular route to accommodate them. *Courtesy of Huguenot-Thomas Paine Historical Association, New Rochelle*

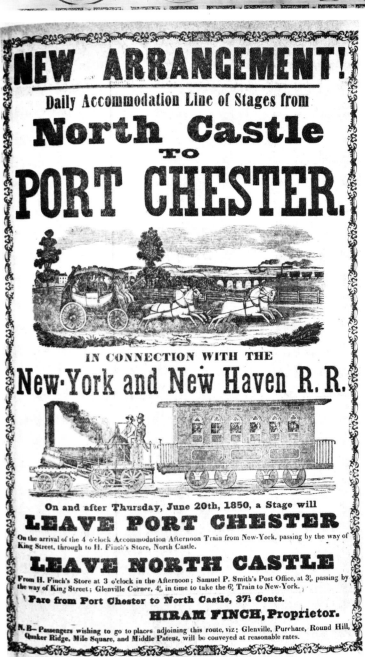

71

Railroad Station, Mamaroneck

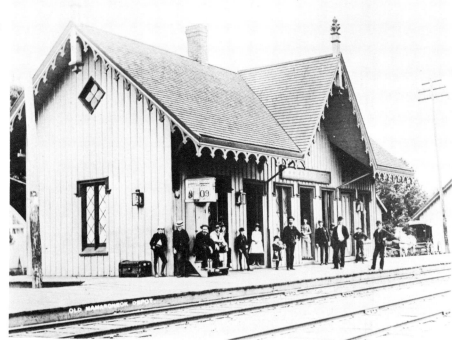

The first railroad station in Mamaroneck, shown as it was in 1898, was typical of the depots in Westchester around the turn of the century. Mamaroneck was forty-five minutes from Grand Central Station on the New Haven line. Commuter rates at the beginning of the twentieth century were $6.00 monthly or fifty individual tickets for $15.30.

The railroad station was a glamorous spot in the evenings when carriages met the trains, especially on Fridays when the Tally-ho was driven down to pick up a wealthy commuter and his weekend guests! Courtesy of Westchester County Historical Society

Neptune House, New Rochelle

Railroads increased the business of Westchester hotels and boarding houses, bringing New York customers to enjoy the services they provided. Between 1830 and 1880 the Neptune House and the LeRoy House were the two most important "public houses," or hotels, in New Rochelle. The proprietor of the Neptune House, located on Neptune Island in the Sound, offered "warm and cold salt and fresh water baths ready at all times.... Pleasure and fishing boats for aquatic excursions, and vehicles and horses for driving or riding provided at a moment's notice" (Nichols, Historic New Rochelle).

The Neptune House was patronized by many New Yorkers, who traveled by boat or stage from Fordham and later by train from the middle of the city. The hotel was torn down around the turn of the century, and Adrian Iselin, who owned the property, presented it to the city of New Rochelle in 1903, to be used as a park. Courtesy of the Old Print Shop, New York

Yorktown Presbyterian Church

The Yorktown Presbyterian Church, on Crompond Road, is built on the site of two previous church buildings. The first, built in 1738, was burned during the Revolution. A new church was built in 1785; that building was replaced by the present church in 1840. Its clean lines reflect the optimistic idealism of Americans in the early nineteenth century. Americans considered their new nation to be the spiritual descendant of the Greek and Roman democracies and celebrated that belief in their architecture. This was especially true of ecclesiastical architecture, and the Yorktown Presbyterian Church is one of the finest examples of this neoclassic style. Photograph by Gray Williams, Jr.

Bolton Priory, Pelham

Religion continued to play an important part in Westchester life, and ministers were valued members of the community. Robert Bolton was born in Savannah, Georgia, in 1788. As a young man, he went to England, where he became a minister. He had thirteen children, so in 1836 he decided to move back to America, believing there were more opportunities for his family here. He became rector of St. Paul's Church, Eastchester, in 1837.

Bolton constructed The Priory, his home in Pelham, in 1838. The date is marked in yellow bricks, brought from the Old Dutch Church in North Tarrytown by Bolton's friend, Washington Irving. Bolton designed his house in the romantic Gothic style and made it appear to have been constructed over a long period of time. The use of stone in some sections and brick in others gives the impression of several additions, although in fact the house looks today much the same as it did in 1838. It is now a private residence. Courtesy of Westchester County Historical Society

Christ the Redeemer Church, Pelham

Soon after Christ Church in Pelham was completed, Robert Bolton resigned from St. Paul's to become rector of the new church. Bolton gave the land on which the church is built. The cornerstone was laid in 1843, and Bolton and his sons did much of the building of the church themselves, including the decorative carving. William Jay Bolton, the rector's son, executed the stained glass windows, the first religious stained glass made in America. Photograph by Janet Wilkins; courtesy of Westchester County Historical Society

73

St. Stephen's Episcopal Church, Armonk

St. Stephen's Episcopal Church was organized in 1842, and the church building was completed the following year. The Reverend Cornelius Winter Bolton, son of Robert Bolton, was rector of St. Stephen's from 1867 until 1880. All five of Robert Bolton's sons were ministers. One of them, Robert, Jr., wrote the first comprehensive history of Westchester County, published in 1848. Cornelius Bolton published a revised second edition of this work in 1881.

St. Stephen's is a handsome example of the neoclassic style very prevalent in Westchester in the mid-nineteenth century. Except for its tower, the church is essentially a Greek temple, rendered in wood. Photograph by Gray Williams, Jr.

Methodist Camp Meeting (1838), Sing Sing

Methodism was extremely popular in this region during the nineteenth century. The first Methodist camp meeting in America was held at Carmel in Putnam County in 1804. It was followed by one at Croton in 1805 and one across the Hudson at Haverstraw in 1825. A camp meeting at Sing Sing in 1831 proved so successful that, in 1834, land was purchased to establish a permanent site for annual meetings.

People attending the two-week summer meetings were housed in small tents. The campground had its own grocery store, post office, and restaurant. Services were held in the afternoon and evening, and special steamboats, and later trains, brought in as many as 10,000 to 15,000 participants. The finale was the "March Around Jerusalem"—the entire congregation marched two by two around the campgrounds, singing hymns. Courtesy of Westchester County Historical Society

Francis Asbury, a pioneer Methodist circuit rider, traveled throughout Westchester in the years just preceding the Revolution. He brought Methodism to Mamaroneck toward the end of 1771. He preached his first service in the village on December 19 and recorded in his journal that "I preached at Mairnock to a company of people who at first took little notice of God, but I trust some of them felt the power of truth in their hearts" (Fulcher, The Story of a Friendly Village).

After the Revolution, Asbury's work in Mamaroneck was carried on under the leadership of Benjamin Griffin, who conducted weekly meetings to prepare men and women for membership in the church. The first Methodist church in Mamaroneck, shown here, was constructed in 1845, on Prospect Avenue near Mamaroneck Avenue. When the congregation outgrew this building, a larger church was built on the Post Road in 1859.

The 1845 church building, which is the oldest structure now standing in Mamaroneck, was used as the town hall for a time and is now occupied by the American Legion. Courtesy of Westchester County Historical Society

Methodist Church, Mamaroneck

Methodist Camp Meeting (1896), Sing Sing

By 1896 the tents of earlier years had been replaced by tiny frame cottages, each with its small plot of flowers. In this picture the children at the camp meeting pose as a group. Note the baby carriage to the right.

Today the campground, located on Camp Woods Road, is a year-round residence for many elderly people, some of whose ancestors founded the camp meeting. Services are still held in the summertime. Courtesy of Ossining Historical Society

Marble School, Eastchester

Westchester towns were divided into school districts when public education laws were enacted by New York State in 1795. Each district had its own small, one-room school-house. The Marble School, located on the corner of Eastchester and California roads in Eastchester, is one of the oldest still standing. It was built in 1835 of marble from the Tuckahoe quarries. The building was originally within what is now the city of Mount Vernon and was moved to its present site in 1869. In 1952 Valentine Kloepfer bequeathed it to the town of Eastchester. The Eastchester Historical Society has restored it and has opened it to the public to demonstrate a typical Victorian school day. Courtesy of Eastchester Historical Society

School Certificate of Merit, Scarsdale

When Hannah Tompkins, who lived and went to school in Scarsdale, earned one of these small, hand-colored slips to show her parents, how proud she must have been! Certificates of merit were awarded students by their teachers for "diligence and good behavior." Courtesy of Westchester County Historical Society

Most children in nineteenth-century Westchester were educated at home or in one-room schools, but there were also private academies established during this period. North Salem Academy was built as a residence by Stephen Delancey about 1770, but he did not complete it. During the Revolution, it was used for a time as a jail and as a courthouse for the trial of "refractory Tories." French troops under General Rochambeau camped for two days in the fields behind the Delancey house in 1782 as they were returning from the Battle of Yorktown.

After the war, the building was purchased by a group of townspeople in North Salem and neighboring communities and completed for use as an academy. It was incorporated in 1790 as the North Salem Academy. It was the first academy in Westchester County and the third in New York State. During its almost 100-year existence there were many notable graduates, among them Daniel D. Tompkins, United States vice-president from 1817 until 1825; DeWitt Clinton, governor of New York; and D. Ogden Mills, a local resident who made a fortune in California during the gold rush days.

The academy was dissolved in 1884 by the New York State legislature when shifting population and the competition with newer schools caused enrollment to decline.

After the academy closed, the building was turned over to the town of North Salem for use as a town hall. Extensive additions were made to the building during the nineteenth century, but it was restored to its early nineteenth-century form in the 1960s. Courtesy of North Salem Historical Society

Bedford Academy and Post Office

The Bedford Academy was built adjacent to the village green in 1807. It was one of Westchester's first classical schools, and many well-known men and women were educated there, among them John Jay II and John McCloskey, the first United States cardinal. Since 1902 the academy building has housed the Bedford Free Library.

The building on the right is the post office, a good example of early nineteenth-century Greek Revival architecture. It formerly stood next to the library but was moved in 1930 when the firehouse was built. The building housed a harness shop for many years and became the village post office around 1900. Courtesy of Westchester County Historical Society

Mount Pleasant Military Academy, Ossining

The Mount Pleasant Academy was established in Sing Sing in 1814 through financial contributions from the community. A Presbyterian minister, the Reverend Thomas Jackson, donated the land. All persons giving five dollars or more became stockholders, and from these contributors, twelve trustees were chosen to run the school. New York Governor Daniel D. Tompkins was one of the first stockholders. The academy was first operated as a day school and proved so successful that in 1834 it moved to larger quarters on Broad Road. Around the middle of the nineteenth century, military schools became popular throughout the country. Proximity to West Point facilitated the change of Mount Pleasant Academy into a military school in 1848. At this time the Female Department, which had been started in 1842 but had not been very successful, was disbanded.

The Mount Pleasant Military Academy remained in operation until 1925. The former library is the only surviving building of the campus; today it serves as a surveyor's office. Courtesy of Westchester County Historical Society

John Jay

Most Westchester citizens were productive but relatively obscure farmers. There were some prominent residents, however; the most notable of these was John Jay. Jay was born in 1745, the son of Peter Jay, a New York City merchant. The Jay family moved to Westchester County in 1746, settling in Rye, although Peter Jay's wife, the former Mary Van Cortlandt, owned land in the Bedford area.

John Jay attended Mr. Stoupe's French school in New Rochelle and was graduated from King's College (now Columbia University) in 1764. He was a prominent member of the Continental Congress, was United States secretary of foreign affairs from 1784 to 1789, and was the first chief justice of the Supreme Court, serving from 1789 to 1795. This portrait of him in his robes as chief justice was painted by Gilbert Stuart in 1794. Jay was then governor of New York from 1795 until he retired in 1801.

Jay had inherited his mother's Bedford land, and it was here that he built his retirement home. He died in 1829. Courtesy of Westchester County Historical Society

Jay Homestead, Katonah

Twenty pounds Reward

Whereas Rails have frequently been taken and carried away from the Subscribers Fences; and several have been lately taken from a Fence near Henry Dickinson's House, the Subscriber will pay the above Reward, on the conviction of the offender, to any Person who shall discover and make known the same to him —

Bedford 17 Sep.r 1802 —   *John Jay —*

"Twenty Pounds Reward"

John Jay was a good neighbor, beloved by his many Westchester friends. Even so respected a man as he, however, had his troubles with local thievery, as this 1802 document indicates. Courtesy of Westchester County Historical Society

John Jay's house at Katonah, built in 1787 as a country retreat, was originally simple and unpretentious. When Jay retired from active life, he took up permanent residence in Westchester and expanded the house considerably. After 1860 Jay's grandson, John Jay II, and subsequent Jay owners, made many further alterations.

When the Jay homestead was acquired by New York State in 1959, the central portion and flanking wings of the house were restored to their appearance in 1801-1829, when John Jay lived there. The other portions of the homestead were left as they were, to reflect the changing tastes of later generations. The home is now open to the public as a New York State Historic Site. Courtesy of Jay Homestead, Katonah

Washington Irving's Sunnyside, Tarrytown

Washington Irving bought a farm on Broadway in Tarrytown in 1835. It had belonged to a branch of the Van Tassel family related to Katrina Van Tassel, whom Irving characterized in his "Legend of Sleepy Hollow."

Irving remodeled a tiny cottage on the property which had been a tenant farmhouse of Philipsburgh Manor known as Wolfert's Roost. Irving renamed the house Sunnyside and described it as "a little, old-fashioned stone mansion, all made up of gable ends, and as full of angles and corners as an old cocked hat" (Sleepy Hollow Restorations, Sunnyside). Over the next twenty years the most prominent literary figures of the day visited Sunnyside, including Nathaniel Hawthorne, Henry Wadsworth Longfellow, and William Cullen Bryant.

Sunnyside's peaceful atmosphere was disrupted when the Hudson River Railroad was constructed between the house and river. Irving was so angry that he complained that "if the Garden of Eden were now on earth they would not hesitate to run a railroad through it." Later the railroad paid Irving $5,000 in damages.

Irving lived at Sunnyside until his death in 1859. His relatives owned the house until 1945, when it was bought by John D. Rockefeller, Jr. Today Sunnyside is owned and operated by Sleepy Hollow Restorations. Courtesy of Sleepy Hollow Restorations

Daniel D. Tompkins

Daniel D. Tompkins, shown here in a portrait by John Wesley Jarvis, was born in Scarsdale in 1774. He attended the North Salem Academy, where he adopted his middle initial to distinguish himself from another Daniel Tompkins at the school. Daniel D. was later graduated from Columbia University and practiced law.

Tompkins was elected governor of New York five times. While governor, he served as commander-in-chief of the New York militia during the War of 1812, which was not a popular cause in the state. President James Madison wanted Tompkins as his vice-president, but Tompkins was too deeply involved in state politics. Had he accepted, he might have become president, rather than James Monroe. He did serve as Monroe's vice-president from 1817 until 1825. He then retired to his home on Staten Island and died soon after, at the age of fifty. Courtesy of Scarsdale Public Library

Elephant Hotel, Somers

ANIMALS, HORSES, &c. at Auction.

On Tuesday and Wednesday, the 22d & 23d of August, instant, at the Elephant Hotel in Somers, will be sold to the highest bidder, all the property and effects of the eastern section of the Zoological Institute.

Conditions of sale, 60 days credit, with approved security, for all sums less than $1000; for all sums of $1000 and upwards, 9 mos. credit with approved security, and interest from the day of sale.—Any person bidding off any of the property shall immediately give such security as may be required.

The sale will commence on Tuesday, at 12 o'clock at noon precisely, with the

Exhibition of Animals

Now in Canada, together with the Horses, Cages, Waggons, Harness, and all the Fixtures and Appurtenances thereto belonging. The Exhibition is now travelling, and possession will be given on the day of sale. The following is a list of the principal Animals, comprising the Exhibition:

The large Elephant VIRGINIUS and Saddle,

1 Dromedary	1 Lion and Lioness	1 Riding Monkey and Poney, with
1 Zebra	1 Leopard	a variety of minor Animals.
1 large white Bear	1 Panther	1 set of Canvass, with poles, chains
1 Royal Tiger	1 striped Hyena	and fixtures complete for immediate use.
1 spotted Hyena	1 Advertising Waggon,

with Horses, Cages, Waggons, &c. sufficient for the use of the Exhibition.——Immediately after the sale of the above Property, will be sold THE CIRCUS which is now travelling with the above Exhibition, consisting of 8 superior Horses, finely marked and well trained to the Ring. Together with all the Saddles, Bridles, Trappings, Wardrobe, and all the appurtenances belonging to Circus Department. After which will be sold,

The rare & valuable Animals now at Somers, together with the Cages and Waggons to which they belong, to wit: the large Male Elephant N.I.M. acknowledged to be the finest elephant ever exhibited in this country, A Female Rhinoceros, a fine healthy animal, with an

One Gnu	One Royal Tiger, Lioness & Black Bear	2 spotted Hyenas
1 Zebra	3 Leopards	1 striped do
2 Royal Tigers	1 Lion and Lioness	1 brown Camel	1 Burmese Bull
2 spotted Tigers, Lion, Lioness & Leopard, 1 cage of small Animals and Birds

Immediately after the sale of the Animals, will be sold a complete set of Canvass with top, sides, poles, chains, guy stakes, and all fixtures complete for immediate use, sufficient to fit up a space of 100 feet in length by 75 feet broad.

The sale will commence on Wednesday the 23d, at Twelve o'clock precisely, with a large number of HORSES, a part of which are

Animal Auction Poster, Somers

Somers and nearby North Salem got caught up in "circus fever" following Hachaliah Bailey's success. A group of North Salem men—John J. June, Lewis B. Titus, Caleb Sutton Angevine, and Jeremiah Crane—formed a syndicate which bought out a business called the Zoological Institute, and the first real "rolling show" was on its way. Many other local families got involved in the new venture, and the buying and selling of exotic animals was not uncommon, as can be seen in this advertisement for an animal auction. Courtesy of Somers Historical Society

The Elephant Hotel in Somers was built between 1820 and 1825 by Hachaliah Bailey. Bailey had purchased an elephant from his sea-captain brother, who had brought the animal back on one of his voyages. Bailey named her Old Bet, took her to Somers, and started a traveling menagerie. It was an important ancestor of the traveling circus.

Old Bet met disaster while the show was in Connecticut. Someone in an angry crowd, who opposed the entertainment on religious grounds, shot and killed the elephant. Bailey had the body stuffed and exhibited in P. T. Barnum's American Museum in New York. A wooden statue of Old Bet stands on a fifteen-foot granite shaft outside the Elephant Hotel, shown here as it appeared in the nineteenth century. The wooden buildings on the right, housing the Farmers and Drovers Bank, were later removed. In 1927 the hotel was acquired by the town of Somers for use as a town hall. Courtesy of Somers Historical Society

D. Ogden Mills' Birthplace, North Salem

One of Westchester's native sons, who "struck it rich" during the California gold rush, was Darius Ogden Mills, born in North Salem in 1825. Mills was educated at the North Salem Academy and at Mount Pleasant Academy in Sing Sing. He went to California in 1848 and made a fortune, not by panning for gold, but by starting a general merchandise business that catered to the gold hunters. Mills later established banks in Sacramento and San Francisco and at his death in 1910 left an estate of $35 million.

Mills maintained a home in New York City as well as an enormous estate in California. He contributed to various philanthropies in New York, among them hotels for the very poor and the Metropolitan Museum of Art. His daughter Elisabeth married Whitelaw Reid, owner of Ophir Hall in Harrison. Mills is buried in Sleepy Hollow Cemetery in North Tarrytown. His birthplace in North Salem appears much as it did when the Mills family occupied it. It is now a private residence. *Courtesy of Westchester County Historical Society*

The Bartow-Pell Mansion was erected on the site of the original manor house of Pelham Manor, probably burned during the Revolution. In 1836 Robert Bartow, a descendant of the Pell and Bartow families, acquired the land and, some time before 1842, built the present mansion in the then-popular Greek Revival style. The architect is not known; both Minard La Fever and John Bolton, son of Robert Bolton, have been credited with the design.

In 1888 the property was purchased by New York City. Then, in 1895, the city annexed a portion of Westchester County, and the Bartow-

Pell mansion, which had been in Pelham Manor, became part of the Bronx.

In 1914 the International Garden Club undertook greatly needed restoration of the mansion and its grounds. Gardens were created to appear as they probably did when the mansion was built. The house is now the headquarters of the International Garden Club and is open to the public. *Courtesy of International Garden Club, the Bronx*

Bartow-Pell Mansion Interior

The Bartow-Pell mansion is a fine example of Greek Revival architecture. The free-standing staircase shown here is an important feature of the house. Since the mansion was built as a country home on a large piece of land, it is on a somewhat larger scale than houses of the same period in New York City. Many of the period furnishings are on loan from museums in New York; others have been donated to the mansion. *Courtesy of Pelham Historical Society*

Bartow-Pell Mansion, The Bronx

Robert Havell, Jr., House, Ossining

Robert Havell, Jr., master engraver and Hudson River School painter, was born in England in 1793. He was hired there by John James Audubon to execute the engravings for Birds of America, *and in 1839 he brought his family to America.*

In 1841 the Havell family moved to Sing Sing and built a home they named Rocky Mount. Havell painted as a hobby but did not sign his works as he wished his reputation to be that of printer and engraver. It was only after his death that he became as well known for his fine landscapes. Rocky Mount still stands on Havell Street although the front porch has been enclosed since this old photograph was taken. Courtesy of Ossining Historical Society

Camp Irving, Tarrytown

Civil War Volunteers, Dobbs Ferry

Westchester County shared in the nation's agony and hardship during the Civil War. Even though most Westchester residents opposed Lincoln and his abolitionist policies, the firing on Fort Sumter on April 12, 1861, found the young men of Westchester eager to be soldiers. It is not known exactly how many men served, but certainly every town and village was represented.

In Dobbs Ferry, with a population of 1,500 in 1861, there were fifty men enlisted. The two pictured here, William McConway and an unidentified companion, are wearing Zouave uniforms. Several regiments, on both sides of the conflict, modeled their uniforms after those of the colorful Zouaves of the French colonial armies. Photograph from Life of a River Village: Dobbs Ferry

Westchester citizens did what they could to aid the soldiers serving in the Union army. At Camp Irving, on the grounds of Jacob Storm's residence in Tarrytown, soldiers from the twenty-sixth Michigan Volunteers, probably a unit of convalescents, camped for a two-week period in October 1863. In a camp journal published in a local newspaper, it was noted that the soldiers were greeted by Captain Storm and made welcome by the local citizens. Lieu-tenant Burch of the Michigan company wrote of their "being received and treated as brothers. Day by day they came—the ladies of Tarrytown—to our sick boys with fruit and flowers and gentle words, with sympathy and Christian counsel" (Scrapbook, Historical Society of the Tarrytowns). Before their departure, the soldiers were given a farewell dinner and presented with a flag made by the girls of the village. Courtesy of Irvington Historical Society

Admiral John Worden

The battle between the ironclads Monitor *and* Merrimac *on March 9, 1862, revolutionized naval warfare. The commander of the* Monitor *was John Lorimer Worden, born in Sparta (now part of Ossining). Worden had served in the navy since 1834. During the battle he was partially blinded by a shell which struck the turret in which he stood. After the war, Worden served as superintendent of the United States Naval Academy from 1869 until 1874. Photograph from* The Soldier in Our Civil War

Admiral David Farragut

David Glasgow Farragut and his wife were both Southerners, but they moved to Hastings in April 1861, leaving the South the day after Virginia seceded. The Farraguts were at first viewed with suspicion by their new Northern neighbors, but when Farragut returned home after his brilliant victories at the Battles of Mobile Bay and New Orleans, Hastings townspeople hung out flags and paraded their now-accepted hero. Farragut was made the first American admiral in 1866, and the family moved away from Hastings in 1869. Photograph from The Soldier in Our Civil War

Lincoln Funeral Arch, Sing Sing

President Lincoln was assassinated six days after Lee surrendered at Appomattox on April 19, 1865. A Westchester man, Elias Bryant, was in Ford's Theatre when the shot rang out. Bryant was one of the first people to rush to the president's aid.

Although Lincoln had not carried Westchester in either the 1860 or 1864 election, local residents were as shocked over the tragedy as the rest of the nation. Stores, churches, and homes were draped in black, and tearful crowds assembled to watch the funeral train pass slowly through the county, traveling from New York to Albany. In Sing Sing, Powles D. Palmer erected a memorial arch across the railroad tracks. Draped in black with American flags, it bore Lincoln's famous words "With charity for all" on its opposite side. Courtesy of Ossining Historical Society

Soldiers' Return, White Plains

At the end of the war, many fewer men returned home than had gone off to fight. Each town celebrated the return of its own soldiers as did White Plains with this parade of veterans.

There was a period of readjustment following the war. A higher cost of living and a glutted labor market meant hard times for many. But

an era of progress and expansion would follow as Westchester families resumed their normal lives once more. Courtesy of White Plains Public Library/Renoda Hoffman

85

Chapter 3

1865-1920:

A Period of Change

The rural way of life was still dominant in most of Westchester in the decades after the Civil War. People led quiet, hard-working lives on their farms or in their villages, their normal routine relieved only by occasional visits to the larger towns. But change was in the air, and by 1914 the lifestyles in Westchester had changed so completely that an 1865 resident would have felt completely out of place. By then railroads, trolleys, automobiles, and paved roads had ended the isolation of Westchester's rugged countryside and opened up the county.

The county shared America's economic prosperity between the Civil War and World War I. Factories and suburbs developed along the Hudson River and in the interior south of White Plains. Thousands of Italians and eastern Europeans came to Westchester in a massive wave of immigration, to build railroads, dams, and mansions and to work in factories. A growing middle class discovered the joys of leisure time. They took "the cars" to boardinghouses and hotels for vacations in the Westchester countryside. Many liked the area and bought gracious shingle and stone homes in the communities built by developers along the railroad lines. By the end of World War I, southern Westchester was an area of towns and growing cities; farms and villages were mostly located north of White Plains. The population had grown from about 100,000 in 1865, to almost 350,000 in 1920.

The New York Central's Putnam and Harlem divisions brought rail service into the north central region of Westchester. No longer did farmers have to make jolting trips by wagon to reach their markets. Once perishable milk products could reach New York City in a few hours by train, dairy farming became big business.

The railroads often determined whether a town grew or declined. In North Salem, a large Methodist church was built in anticipation of the growth expected when the railroad came through. But instead, the station was built at Purdys, a few miles to the west, and the church sat half-empty on Sundays. Three unsuccessful attempts were made to bring the railroad to Pound Ridge, and, when Somers voted against having the railroad come through the town, manufacturers, other businesses, and the Farmers and Drovers Bank all moved to Mount Kisco. By 1895 Mount Kisco, which had consisted of only four buildings in 1847, was a town bustling with factories and summer hotels. In both Chappaqua and Yorktown, the town centers shifted as businesses and stores relocated to be near the train station.

It was not long after the old Croton Dam was completed in 1842

New York Central Railroad Engine
Courtesy of Westchester County Historical Society

that New York City made plans to build more dams and reservoirs in Westchester. Between the 1880s and the 1920s the Kensico, Croton, and Catskill water systems were constructed. The flooding of thousands of acres for these reservoirs created considerable dislocations in many towns north of White Plains. The building of the New Croton Dam and its reservoirs, for instance, forced the complete relocation of the village of Katonah to higher ground and the construction of thirty-two miles of new roads and nineteen new bridges. Legal proceedings on 600 land condemnations for the New Croton Dam dragged on for thirteen years. Many factories and mills, which lost their waterpower when streams were diverted for the water system, had to relocate or went out of business. In North Salem, the hamlet of Purdys was moved, and 5 percent of the town was inundated, including hundreds of prime acres of dairy land.

The Kensico Water System was constructed in the 1880s. It included the Kensico Dam and the Byram Lake Dam; and it drew water from Little and Big Rye ponds and Wampus Lake. More water was brought to New York through the Croton Water System, developed between 1892 and 1907, which included the Titicus Dam, Muscoot Dam, Amawalk Reservoir, and a larger Croton Dam.

After New York incorporated the boroughs of the Bronx, Brooklyn, Queens, and Staten Island in 1898, the water supply had to be increased again. Plans for the Catskill Water System were approved by the state of New York, and between 1906 and 1915 more dams and reservoirs were built to bring an additional 500 million gallons of water a day to New York City. Water from the new reservoirs west of the Hudson had to be carried through Westchester by way of a new aqueduct which led to the new reservoir created behind a larger Kensico Dam, completed in 1915. By 1924 New York City owned 18,320 acres of land in fourteen Westchester towns. And still New York thirsted. The Delaware Water System, completed in 1944, increased New York's water supply by 800 million gallons a day from four reservoirs on the south slope of the Catskill Mountains.

In the last half of the nineteenth century, Westchester's proximity to New York City, its transportation systems, and its available labor force attracted many manufacturing concerns, particularly along the Hudson River. Peekskill and Croton continued to be centers for the iron industry. Some factories established at this time were Standard Oilcloth (later Standard Textile Products) in Buchanan; Mobile Company of America (later the General Motors Assembly Plant) in North Tarrytown; Lord and Burnham Greenhouse Manufacturing Company in Irvington; Hudson River Brewing Company in Dobbs Ferry; Zinsser Chemical, Hastings Pavement, and National Conduit (later Anaconda) Manufacturing Company in Hastings; and Otis Elevator and Alexander Smith Carpet Company in Yonkers.

In this period, more and more people were anxious to move out of New York City to the suburbs. Communities were laid out in southern Westchester where farms had stood a generation earlier. As the population grew, villages and towns became incorporated, and taxes were collected to provide necessary public services, such as paved roads, sewers, fire companies, and police forces. Horse-drawn trolley lines were established throughout the county in the 1880s and were electrified by 1890. Steamboats continued to do a brisk freight and

Hopper's Grocery, White Plains
Courtesy of Westchester County Historical Society

passenger business on the Hudson River and Long Island Sound right up to World War I. For twenty-five cents one could take a day trip on a Starin steamboat from New York to the internationally-famous Starin's Glen Island Resort in New Rochelle.

People who were freed from the seven-day-a-week commitment to farmwork began to participate in all kinds of sports and recreational activities. Tennis, golf, baseball, canoeing, and bicycling grew in popularity. Wintertime activities included sleigh rides and tobogganing. In the days before ice-cutters, the Hudson River often froze from bank to bank, and hundreds enjoyed skating and ice boating on its surface. In the summer, vacationers flocked to the beaches of New Rochelle and Rye or to the lakes and hills of northern Westchester. The wealthy joined exclusive clubs such as the Larchmont and American Yacht clubs to participate in the new sport of ocean sailboat racing. Automobile clubs were formed for family outings, and it was not long before the first automobile races were run. In 1908 Walter Law staged the American International Race for Stock Cars. Thousands of spectators lined the thirty-five-mile course to watch twenty-two drivers career along unpaved roads for a $10,000 prize.

The period after 1865 brought vast fortunes to a new class of entrepreneurs in the New York area. Many built large estates in Westchester County. Colonial, Chateauesque, and Renaissance Revival houses were built on the hills overlooking the Hudson River and Long Island Sound. Perhaps the most fantastic of all were the homes built to resemble castles, such as Lyndhurst in Tarrytown, Ophir Hall in Purchase, Leland Castle in New Rochelle, and Carroll-cliff (now Axe Castle) in Tarrytown. In northern Westchester, magnificent mansions were built on the hilltops of New Castle, Bedford, and North Castle.

None of the estates, however, matched the grandeur and scope of the Rockefeller estates. The largest mansion in the county was the 204-room Rockwood Hall, built by William Rockefeller in 1887 on 1,000 acres overlooking the Hudson River in North Tarrytown and Mount Pleasant. William's brother, John D. Rockefeller, completed his mansion and gardens on 3,500 acres in Pocantico Hills in 1913. His son raised his family of six children there and built a million-dollar recreation hall that included a bowling alley, squash court, tennis court, and swimming pool. John D., Sr., enjoyed playing golf daily on his own course built on the grounds, and when the Putnam railroad disturbed his peace, he persuaded the railroad to move its tracks five miles away.

In the years around World War I, Westchester joined the suffragette movement with vigor. By 1915 *Westchester Life of To-Day* reported that 20,000 women were enrolled in the suffrage cause, which had 102 clubs organized by assembly and election districts. In 1917 the New York legislature voted to give women the right to vote in state affairs, and in August 1920, Westchester's suffragettes celebrated the successful passage of the Nineteenth Amendment to the Constitution.

In 1914 Westchester residents anxiously watched the beginning of World War I, and when the United States joined the conflict, many Westchester men stepped forward to take part. Within a month, for

Genehurst, Dobbs Ferry
Courtesy of Dobbs Ferry Historical Society

example, twenty-eight Dobbs Ferry men had enlisted in the armed services. Home Defense leagues and Liberty Loan committees were formed in every town; women joined the Red Cross, farmed community gardens, and operated canteens. The village of Scarsdale prepared for civilian unrest by purchasing twenty riot guns and surveyed homes for guns and aliens. Thursdays and Sundays were designated as "lightless nights," to save coal for the war emergency.

For army units assigned to guard the dams and aqueducts, however, duty was not always arduous. "We're living like millionaires up here," stated Corporal Gerard of Company L's Tenth Regiment, which had been assigned to Shaft Nine of the aqueduct on the Rockefeller estate. John D. Rockefeller supplied the soldiers daily with eggs, sandwiches, coffee, and a cooking stove.

As the war drew to a close, Westchester celebrated Armistice Day with parades and church services. In Dobbs Ferry, Miss Masters marched the girls of the Masters School to the Presbyterian Church, where, after a brief service, they paraded through the village singing "Onward Christian Soldiers." ∎

After 1865, rural life continued unchanged in the northern part of Westchester County. Life seemed to pass as slowly as the water in this brook in Dobbs Ferry on a summer's day in the late 1800s. Here the girl on the bank waits patiently as her brother carries their little sister across the stream. Photograph from Dobbs Ferry: Life of a River Village

Children in a Brook, Dobbs Ferry

Delivering the Mail in North Salem

Horse and Buggy, Bedford

Mrs. Coopernail of Bedford poses with her dog in the horse and buggy so familiar on Westchester's country roads during the second half of the nineteenth century. Her surgeon husband, Dr. George Coopernail, was one of the founders of the Northern Westchester Hospital in Mount Kisco. He was known as the "horse-and-buggy doctor" until 1910, when he purchased an open Maxwell for his calls. Courtesy of Westchester County Historical Society

Catching the Mail at Scarborough Station

Theodore Neidi, the Scarborough postmaster, stands on a ladder ready to catch the local mail from a Hudson River Railroad train in the early 1900s. Mailbags were caught by the iron arm as the express trains passed by. Mail delivery was revolutionized by the railroads. Courtesy of Briarcliff Manor/Scarborough Historical Society

In the rural areas of the county, mail delivery was often delayed by poor roads and bad weather. In a photograph taken about 1905, a woman, possibly the minister's wife, reaches for her letter in front of the Universalist Church.

Today the church has been remodeled as a private residence, owned by the North Salem postmaster. Courtesy of Richard DeFrances, North Salem Historian

One-room School, Chappaqua

Well into the twentieth century the more rural areas of Westchester continued to depend upon one-room schoolhouses like this one in Chappaqua. Even today, residents like Leonard Scofield of Pound Ridge can recall the smell of drying mittens over the pot-bellied stove and the excitement of performing the Christmas pageant by candlelight for their parents. As communities grew, one-room schools became obsolete and were replaced by community elementary schools which enjoyed individual classrooms and central heating. Courtesy of Chappaqua Historical Society

Hickory-Stick Discipline, Bedford

Discipline was often dealt with a hard blow to the area being massaged by the unhappy young man at the front desk. His desk-mate appears unconcerned, but a word of encouragement is being whispered from behind a book by a friend. Perhaps the spanking was administered because the boy drew an unflattering picture of the teacher on the schoolroom wall. Courtesy of Bedford Historical Society

Ardsley Public School Picnic

A school picnic at the end of the year was a special treat, anticipated for months by children at the Ardsley elementary school. Here they pose for a class picture on Wyman's Rock in Ardsley in the 1890s. Courtesy of Barbara Novich

Chappaqua Mountain Institute

The Chappaqua Mountain Institute was one of several private schools and seminaries founded in Westchester in the last half of the nineteenth century. It was built in 1870 to educate Quaker children, many of whom boarded there. An 1875 catalogue listed "tuition, board and washing" at $250 per year. During the summer months, the institute operated as a boarding-house, as indicated by the "Season Opens June 23rd" note on this postcard.

The original building burned in 1885, was rebuilt, and, in 1908, was presented to the Children's Aid Society by Elizabeth Milbank Anderson. It was used as a convalescent home for children for many years and was demolished after a fire in the late 1970s. Courtesy of Chappaqua Historical Society

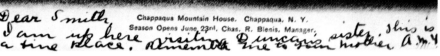

Pleasantville High School Band

Pleasantville High School, in 1913, formed the first high school band in New York State. This group of band musicians posed proudly in June 1918. The band included a bass violin in addition to the customary wind and brass instruments and drums.

The band was the inspiration of Pleasantville Superintendent of Schools John Morgan. He sold the idea of the community, which backed it enthusiastically and raised money for uniforms and instruments. Standing in the background is Fred Quinlan, the school's music teacher, who was responsible for the band's musical instruction.

Pleasantville High School was located at that time on Bedford Road, in the building which contains the current elementary school. Courtesy of John Crandall, Pleasantville Historian

Basket Maker

Pound Ridge was known for its basket-making. The center of the activity was the hamlet of Scotts Corners, sometimes called Basket Town, and also neighboring Dantown, where the baskets were known as Dantown crockery. The baskets were made entirely by hand, a process that began with the splitting of white oak logs. The split logs were stored under water through the winter, then shaved into splints which were pounded until they were pliable enough to be woven. A skilled worker could make six two-bushel baskets a day. Seen here is Lincoln Jones of Pound Ridge, hard at work at his craft.

The peak for the basket-making industry came just after the Civil War, when Pound Ridge baskets were extensively used in the oyster industry around New York City and in Long Island Sound. By the end of the nineteenth century, increased harbor pollution caused oystering to decline, which in turn caused the demise of the basket industry. Courtesy of Pound Ridge Historical Society

Basket Rack

This wagon, or "basket rack," hung with forty or fifty dozen baskets, was used to carry finished baskets to market. One of the best-known sellers of baskets was "Blind Charlie" Scofield, who had lost his eyesight at seven from scarlet fever. He could make baskets as well as anyone and with a young boy as pilot drove the basket rack between Poughkeepsie and New Haven. Courtesy of Pound Ridge Historical Society

By the end of the nineteenth century, shoemaking was completely carried on in factory buildings rather than at home as a cottage industry. Here the shoemakers of the Isreal and Zarr Company take a break from their work to pose in their leather aprons for the cameraman. This picture was taken in the 1880s.

The factory building, sometimes known as Century House, was originally located on the north side of Bedford Road in Pleasantville. It served as the residence of Amos Clark for a time and was torn down in the 1940s or 1950s. Courtesy of John Crandall, Pleasantville Historian

Shoe Factory, Pleasantville

Mr. Brundage, Blacksmith, Armonk

Harry M. Brundage, photographed here at his blacksmith's forge, was a familiar sight in North Castle for many years. The Brundage family had come to North Castle from Rye as early as 1696 and later owned more than 1,000 acres of land in the town. Harry Brundage began working in the blacksmith's shop, located on the corner of Greenwich Road and Route 22, in 1895, when he was only sixteen. He was still working five-and-a-half days a week in 1954 when he died beside his anvil at the age of seventy-five. Demands for horseshoeing had been slow for quite some time, but Mr. Brundage kept himself busy making andirons and fireplace screens, hinges, and other hardware. He was an institution in North Castle, sorely missed when he was gone.

After Mr. Brundage died, his blacksmith shop was taken down and reassembled on the Cerak farm in Silver Lake. In 1981 the Cerak family gave the building to the North Castle Historical Society. It has been moved back to North Castle, where it has become part of the North Castle Historical Society's museum complex at Smith's Tavern. Courtesy of North Castle Historical Society

Playing Marbles at Crolly's Store, Pleasantville

Time stood still as a businessman paused in front of Crolly's store in Pleasantville to show the local boys his skill at shooting marbles. Courtesy of John Crandall, Pleasantville Historian

Westchester County Fair Racetrack

Rural fairs have been held in Westchester since 1690, when the New York provincial government directed that two annual fairs be held in the area, one at the Borough of Westchester (now part of the Bronx) and the other at Bedford. In the nineteenth century the most popular fairs were held at the old fairgrounds on Tarrytown Road in Greenburgh. Annual fairs were held here from 1885 until 1922. The fairgrounds covered more than fifty acres and included gardens, exhibition halls, barns, and a racetrack. Shown here is a race during the fair held in 1897.

Chief booster of the fair was Edward B. Long, a White Plains newspaperman and state fair commissioner. When he died in 1924, the family sold off the land on which the fairgrounds stood. From 1935 until 1950 the Westchester Horticultural Society held annual fairs under the old charter, at the County Center in White Plains, but these were really flower shows rather than the old-time county fairs. Courtesy of Westchester County Historical Society

Judging Vegetables at the Westchester County Fair

Here are the tables of produce that Westchester farmers and gardners entered in the competition for blue ribbons at the 1893 fair. Note the pumpkins on the last table. Courtesy of Westchester County Historical Society

First Engine on the Putnam Line, Somers

The engineer and his men stood proudly on the first engine of the Putnam division of the New York Central Railroad which was constructed in 1880-81. The railroad connected the Sixth Avenue and Ninth Avenue elevated roads at 155th Street in New York City with stops through central Westchester, ending at Baldwin Place in Somers. This picture, taken in 1880, is of the Mahopac branch. Note the turntable used to reverse the direction of the engine. Many Westchester commuters still fondly remember the old "Put," which stopped running in 1958. Courtesy of Somers Historical Society

Cattle Herd at Briarcliff Lodge

In 1890 Walter W. Law purchased the 400-acre Whitson farm near Sparta, planning to develop a model of modern agricultural practices. It was the beginning of Briarcliff Farms, which by 1901 encompassed 6,000 acres, a herd of 1,645 head of Jersey cattle, a dairy, greenhouses, and the School of Practical Agriculture and Horticulture. Law's objective was "to produce pure food of the highest standard of excellence." These high standards brought top prices for Briarcliff dairy products in New York City and its suburbs.

A New York Tribune article in May 1901 stated that Mr. Law made sure that his cattle never heard a "harsh or offensive word; kindess and gentleness characterize every motion of the attendants." Cleanliness was a byword and the barns were kept "as free from odor as any room in a private house." People paid as much as ten cents a quart for milk from happy Briarcliff Farms cows.

The most famous product of the Briarcliff greenhouses was the "Briarcliff Rose." Eight thousand American Beauty roses were picked daily from 100,000 plants and sold in New York City and around the world.

Briarcliff Farms evolved into the community of Briarcliff Manor. Walter Law built the Congregational Church, the Briarcliff Manor Light and Power Company, the Briarcliff Laundry, and the Briarcliff Table Water Company, which bottled pure water "from the reservoirs of creation." Courtesy of Briarcliff Manor/Scarborough Historical Society

Bottling Plant at Briarcliff Farms

The Briarcliff Farms bottling plant was a model of cleanliness and efficiency. Three thousand to four thousand quarts of milk a day were processed and sent to New York City on the Putnam Railroad.

The availability of daily train transport made possible large dairying operations like Briarcliff Farms. Courtesy of Briarcliff Manor/Scarborough Historical Society

Great Barn Fire at Briarcliff Farms

On April 28, 1913, this spectacular fire took place at the Briarcliff Farms barn on Dalmeny Road in Briarcliff Manor. St. Theresa's School now occupies the site. Courtesy of Briarcliff Manor/Scarborough Historical Society

Briarcliff Lodge

Briarcliff Lodge became the most exclusive hotel in Westchester County in the 1920s. The hotel catered to the wealthy who considered a stay at the lodge a must on their way to Lake Mohonk for the summer season. Mrs. Stewart White, who rented an entire wing at the lodge, paid $10,000 for the season in 1915.

Guests enjoyed the fresh products of Briarcliff Farms, a superb view of the Hudson River, and "a sense of comfort as in the best-appointed home." U.S. Olympic hopeful Johnny Weismuller trained here in 1924 in what was then the world's largest outdoor swimming pool. In 1926 snow was brought down from Canada for the U.S. Olympic ski-jump trials held on a platform built in front of the lodge.

Briarcliff Lodge serves today as the administration building of King's College. Courtesy of King's College, Briarcliff Manor

Blizzard of '88, North Salem

Sometimes rural tranquility could be interrupted by natural catastrophies. "Now we all know just what a blizzard is." This headline in a Westchester newspaper of March 1888 hints of the swapping of stories that must have taken place in every Westchester town after the worst snowstorm the county ever knew—tales, not of shoveling paths, but of digging ditches and tunnels through drifts several feet deep. Bitter cold and fierce winds helped to create conditions that virtually shut down every community for several days.

While only twenty-one inches of snowfall was recorded in Westchester on March 12, wind velocity was forty miles per hour, and gusts were measured at eighty-five miles per hour. The winds created drifts which halted all traffic, mail and milk deliveries, and train service for more than two days. It must have been a welcome sight in North Salem when the first train, pictured above, made it through. Courtesy of North Salem Historical Society

Tornado in Chappaqua

A rare natural disaster struck the Quaker settlement in Chappaqua when a cyclone touched down on July 16, 1904. In only ten minutes the tornado had flattened six houses, uprooted countless trees, injured twenty people, and killed Mrs. Washburn, who was too elderly to leave her home. In this photograph, strolling sightseers along Quaker Road survey the damage. Courtesy of Chappaqua Historical Society

Workers on the New Croton Dam

Even before the Kensico Dam was completed in 1885, it had become apparent that the water supply to New York would have to be increased. In 1893 work began on the New Croton Dam in Croton Gorge in the town of Cortlandt.

Under the padrone system about 2,000 men, brought from southern Italy, agreed to work a ten-hour day for $1.35. The village constructed for the workers was called The Bowery and included twelve saloons, twenty-three hotels and boardinghouses, a barber shop, two general stores, and three "houses of assignation." It took fourteen years to complete the dam. Many of the laborers' families were able to join them and then settled permanently in the area. Courtesy of the Ossining Historical Society

Construction Strike at the New Croton Dam

In April 1900 the workers on the New Croton Dam demanded a pay increase to $1.50 for an eight-hour day. The contractors refused to pay, saying they could not afford the increase, so the workers went on strike.

The National Guard was called in to prevent violence. Their tent camp is seen in this photograph, with the unfinished dam in the center.

The New York Water Commissioners met and decreed that the increase must be paid. This ended the strike, but it was seven more years before the dam was completed. Courtesy of the Westchester County Historical Society

Moving a House in Katonah

In order to create the new Croton Water System, 600 parcels of land were condemned, including the entire village of Katonah. After losing a bitter legal battle with the city of New York to prevent the inundation of their village, Katonah residents decided to move the town. The Katonah Land Company bought twenty-five acres across the river and a half-mile to the southwest. Commercial and residential plots were sold to the residents and, as a contemporary newspaper noted, "the wandering village is off; a great chance for the sportsman who would prove he can hit a flock of barns!"

About 1,000 people were forced to leave. About 100 buildings were moved; the others were torn down. Even the cemetery was relocated.

In this photograph, taken about 1895, the Chapman house has been hoisted on a crib of timbers, and the horse is ready to operate the windlass which will slowly slide the house along on oak rails to its new site. The houses inched along so slowly that residents often remained living in them. This may have been the case here, as evidenced by the laundry hanging on the porch. Courtesy of Bedford Historical Society

New Croton Dam, Croton

Workers on the Aqueduct, Millwood

In 1907 the New Croton Dam was finally finished. Stone for it had been brought from the Rudinger quarry, five miles east of Peekskill, on a special railroad constructed for the purpose.

The completed dam is over 200 feet high. Croton Reservoir has a capacity of about 34 billion gallons of water, and the watershed covers 375 square miles. Nevertheless, it is small indeed compared with the great Catskill and Delaware water systems that would later be impounded to serve New York's thirst. Courtesy of Richard Lederer, Jr. Scarsdale Historian

The Catskill Aqueduct, completed in 1917, went through the towns of Cortlandt, Yorktown, New Castle, Mount Pleasant, Greenburgh, and Yonkers. The entire water system included ten new dams and reservoirs and brought 500 million gallons of water per day down the ninety-three miles from the Ashokan Reservoir near Kingston to the Hillview Reservoir by Yonkers Raceway.

This photograph, taken about 1915, shows Italian laborers working on the huge concrete pipes of the new aqueduct which carries water from the reservoirs to New York City. Courtesy of Ruth Allen Kniffen

Elizabeth Stevenson, of Croton-on-Hudson, employed many of the skilled Italian stone-masons who had built the New Croton Dam and Aqueduct. Mrs. Stevenson had inherited property bounded by the Old Post Road, Prospect Place, North Riverside Avenue, and Stevenson Place in Croton-on-Hudson.

Over the next forty years, she and her architect son Harvey designed a unique enclave of twenty stone houses surrounded by a forty-foot-high stone wall. The houses were sold or rented to friends, many of whom were professionals in the arts, including: etcher Ernest Haskell, painter Kenyon Cox, actor Paul Valentine, and Jeanette Dexter, a dancer at the Irma Duncan School in Finney Farm in Croton. (Irma was Isadora Duncan's sister.) An auditorium with a large stage was built in the Dexter home for dance performances.

Mrs. Stevenson played Italian operas on her Victrola for the workers building the houses, and they responded by using their talents to the fullest. Stone was used to regrade the property and to build the walled platform on which the enclave stands. Romantic stone loggias and gazebos graced the center garden around which the buildings were arranged.

The houses still stand on the Old Post Road in Croton-on-Hudson. *Courtesy of Historical Reference Room, Croton-on-Hudson Public Library*

Elizabeth Stevenson, Creator of the Stevenson Houses, Croton

Wyndhurst, Croton-on-Hudson

Wyndhurst was designed for Elizabeth Stevenson and her husband Frederick by Percy Griffen of New York. The thirty-room mansion of stone and brick is of a rather eclectic Medieval Revival style. Wyndhurst later became the home of Harold Gray, creator of Little Orphan Annie. At one time the house was known as Ann Robinson's Sunshine Farm and was used as a rest home for alcoholic women.

Today Wyndhurst is a private residence. Courtesy of Westchester County Historical Society

Columbus Statue, White Plains

The Stella d'Italia Society was proud of its Italian heritage and the contributions of Italians to America and Westchester County. The society commissioned this ten-ton, six-foot statue of Christopher Columbus, made of Carrara marble from Italy. The statue was erected on Broadway at Lake Street in White Plains.

Mr. Rocco Briante, president of the Stella d'Italia Society, presented the statue to the city of White Plains on October 12, 1915.

In 1954 the statue was moved eighty-five feet north of its original site to its present location on the esplanade of Broadway near the corner of Barker Avenue. Courtesy of Westchester County Historical Society

Kensico Dam and Plaza, Valhalla

The new Kensico Dam was built between 1906 and 1915, directly north of the old Kensico Dam at Valhalla, to contain the 500 million gallons of water brought to its reservoir each day from the Catskill Water System. The water level in the reservoir rose 100 feet above the level contained in the old reservoir before the additional water supply was added. This necessitated the moving of the village of Kensico, known in colonial days as Wright's Mills.

The contractor provided housing for 1,500 workers. Rock for the dam was brought by railroad from Quarry Heights in Harrison. Sand came from east of Rye Lake. More concrete was made at the dam site, and made faster, than for the construction of the Panama Canal.

The dam was completed in 1915 and a beautiful park, Kensico Dam Plaza, was developed in front of it by Westchester County. The plaza has been the site of many flea markets, festivals, and other public events ever since its opening in the 1920s. Courtesy of the Westchester County Department of Parks, Recreation and Conservation

Rendering of New Kensico Dam Plaza

The Westchester County Department of Parks, Recreation and Conservation has developed a plan to renovate the Kensico Dam Plaza in the 1980s. Shown here is a rendering of the projected renovation. Courtesy of Westchester County Department of Parks, Recreation and Conservation

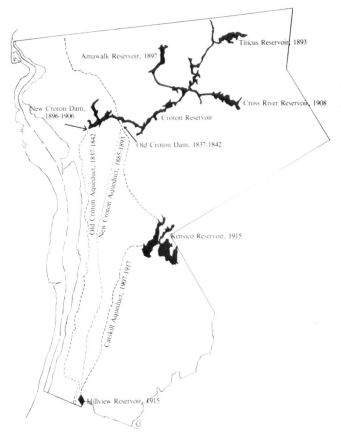

Map of Dams, Reservoirs, and Aqueducts in Westchester County

Photograph from Sanchis, American Architecture: *Westchester County*

Naylor Brothers Foundry Workers, Peekskill

From early in the nineteenth century, iron foundries were an important industry in Peekskill. Stove works and plow works thrived until the Civil War cut off the sale of plows to the South; the stove works survived until 1931. This photograph of workers at the Naylor Brothers Iron and Brass Foundry and Machine Shop was taken in 1952. Courtesy of Field Library, Peekskill

Abendroth Iron Foundry, Port Chester

Industrialization, spurred by the railroads and an expanding labor force, proceeded rapidly in Westchester County following the Civil War. William A. Abendroth established the Abendroth Iron Foundry in the 1840s in Port Chester, along the Byram River at Mill and Main streets. By 1885 the foundry ranked as one of the largest on the East Coast and was the largest employer in Port Chester. Its stoves and furnaces were shipped all over the world. Courtesy of Port Chester Public Library

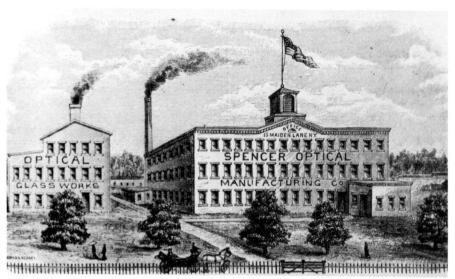

Spencer Optical Company, Mount Kisco

The town of Mount Kisco developed as a direct result of the railroad. Factories established there included a cotton factory, which produced cotton batting for the Union army during the Civil War, and a needle factory.

The Spencer Optical Works, pictured here, was recruited from New Haven by the Mount Kisco town fathers in 1874. The town paid to build the factory on the Kisco River near Kirbyville. At its peak it employed 200 people and was the largest spectacle factory in the world, producing 550,000 pairs a year.

In 1889 the factory closed and moved to Newark, New Jersey. The mill's water supply was reduced when Kirby pond was drained to end a malaria outbreak. Courtesy of Westchester County Historical Society

Mobile Company of America, North Tarrytown

The Mobile Company of America began producing Walker Steam cars in the summer of 1900 in this impressive 700-window factory, designed by Stanford White on the former Kingsland estate in North Tarrytown. From 1904 to 1913 the Maxwell-Briscoe Motor Company owned the plant, which employed 2,000. By 1912 Maxwell-Briscoe led the world in the production of low-priced automobiles. The company sold the factory in 1915 to Chevrolet, which used it as an assembly plant. Cars are still produced at this site, which is now part of the large General Motors assembly plant. Courtesy of Historical Society of the Tarrytowns

Otis Elevator Company, Yonkers

For many decades one of Yonkers's largest employers has been the Otis Elevator Company. Motor-driven elevators had been used for many years to lift freight when Elisha G. Otis of Yonkers designed a safety brake and the elevator was considered safe enough to carry people. He began commercial production in 1853.

The passenger elevator pictured here carried about 10,000 persons in three days when it was installed in the Lord and Taylor's store in New York City about 1870. It had seats for passengers and was operated by steam.

Today the huge complex of Otis Elevator Company buildings stretches from Larkin Plaza to Ashburton Avenue and from Woodworth Avenue to the Hudson River. Courtesy of Hudson River Museum, Yonkers

Alexander Smith Carpet Mills, Yonkers

The Alexander Smith Carpet Mills started as a small business in West Farms (now part of the Bronx) in 1845. After two fires, Smith moved his business to Yonkers, reopening in 1865 in a building on the Saw Mill River formerly occupied by the Waring Hat Company. With the aid of his partner, Halycon Skinner, Smith invented a power loom that revolutionized the carpet industry. The Axminster loom enabled the carpet mill to increase production tenfold, and by the end of the century the Alexander Smith Company was the largest carpet manufacturer in the world. The mill buildings grew to cover sixty-seven acres of floor space, and at the peak of production 7,600 people were employed. Many of these people were European immigrants, largely of Ukrainian, Polish, and Slavic background.

The mills were at their most prosperous during World War II, when they operated twenty-four hours a day making canvas tents and blankets for the war effort. During the 1950s, however, labor and other costs became much higher; the mills began to lose money, and in 1954 the entire operation was moved to Mississippi.

The mill buildings have since all been sold to other businesses. Nearly 100 firms occupy the forty-seven buildings of the Smith Company, and many of the workers who lost their jobs when the Smith Carpet Mills moved south have found new employment in their old place of work.

This photograph, taken in the 1930s, shows women working inside the factory. Coutesy of Hudson, River Museum, Yonkers

North Broadway, Yonkers, N. Y.

North Broadway, Yonkers

This view was taken along North Broadway in Yonkers in 1896. The factories, which had been erected along the Hudson River between 1870 and 1895, had attracted large numbers of western European laborers, mostly Irish, German, and Scots. Despite the loss of the Kingsbridge section to the Bronx in 1874, the population of Yonkers had doubled from 20,000 to 40,000 between 1872 and 1890. After World War I, many immigrants from eastern Europe came to work in these industrial plants, including large numbers of Ukrainians who fled the communist takeover of their homeland. Courtesy of Westchester County Historical Society

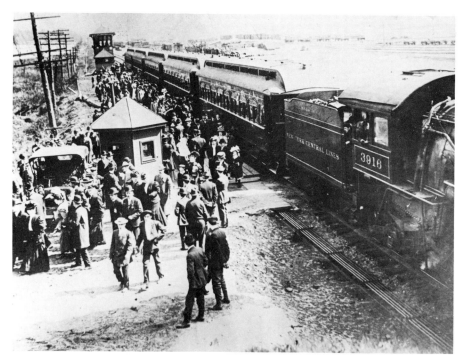

Harmon Station

Clifford B. Harmon was a New York real estate developer with a dream—a dream that for a time came true. Harmon's opportunity came when the New York Central Railroad decided to electrify the Hudson Line from Croton south. Harmon figured this would make the small town a major express stop, so in 1903 he sold some of the land he had bought from the Van Cortlandt family to the railroad. In the deed he specified that the station must always be called Harmon and that every train must stop there.

He then set out to develop the village of Harmon, a residential community encouraging theater and arts. He received considerable help from Lillian Nordica, a popular opera singer at the turn of the century. Elegant houses, a theater, and two Japanese teahouses, the Mikado and the Nikko, were part of a plan to entice leaders in the theatrical and musical world to establish themselves in the new community. Harmon ran special trains like this one from New York to bring prospective buyers to his new town.

At first the community appeared to be a success, but the death of Miss Nordica and the advent of World War I in 1914 brought the end of Mr. Harmon's dream. He spent little time in Westchester thereafter and became better known as an aviator. Courtesy of History Reference Room, Croton-on-Hudson Public Library

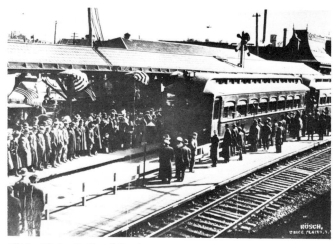

White Plains Railroad Station

By 1912, when this picture was taken, White Plains had developed into a bustling city, and the railroad provided an essential service by bringing residents to and from the county seat. Courtesy of White Plains Public Library/Renoda Hoffman

Orawaupum Hotel, White Plains

The Daily Grind

Problems with unsatisfactory train service have been plaguing commuters for a long time, as indicated by this 1907 cartoon from the N.Y. Globe and Commercial Advertiser. Courtesy of Huguenot-Thomas Paine Historical Association, New Rochelle

The Orawaupum Hotel, located on Railroad Avenue and Orawaupum Street and photographed here in 1897, was typical of the hotels built to accommodate railroad travelers.

The first Orawaupum Hotel, built in 1844, was named for one of the Indian chiefs who signed the deed for the lands that became White Plains. When the building burned in 1854, a second hotel was built by Mrs. Margaret A. Smith. During her ownership it became one of the better-known hotels in White Plains.

The Orawaupum Hotel was the location for the organizational meetings of the founders of the Westchester County Historical Society in 1874. Courtesy of White Plains Public Library / Renoda Hoffman

Park Hill Elevator, Yonkers

Park Hill in Yonkers was one of the 1890s housing developments planned along the commuter railroads by real estate companies. Large stone and shingle homes, graced by towers and elegant landscaping, attracted well-to-do businessmen who wanted both comfortable homes for their families and easy access to New York City.

Pictured here is the elevator which brought commuters up the hill from the railroad station. Comfortable waiting rooms were built at each end of the cog-style elevator. They still stand, as private residences, but the elevator is long gone. Courtesy of Huguenot-Thomas Paine Historical Association, New Rochelle

107

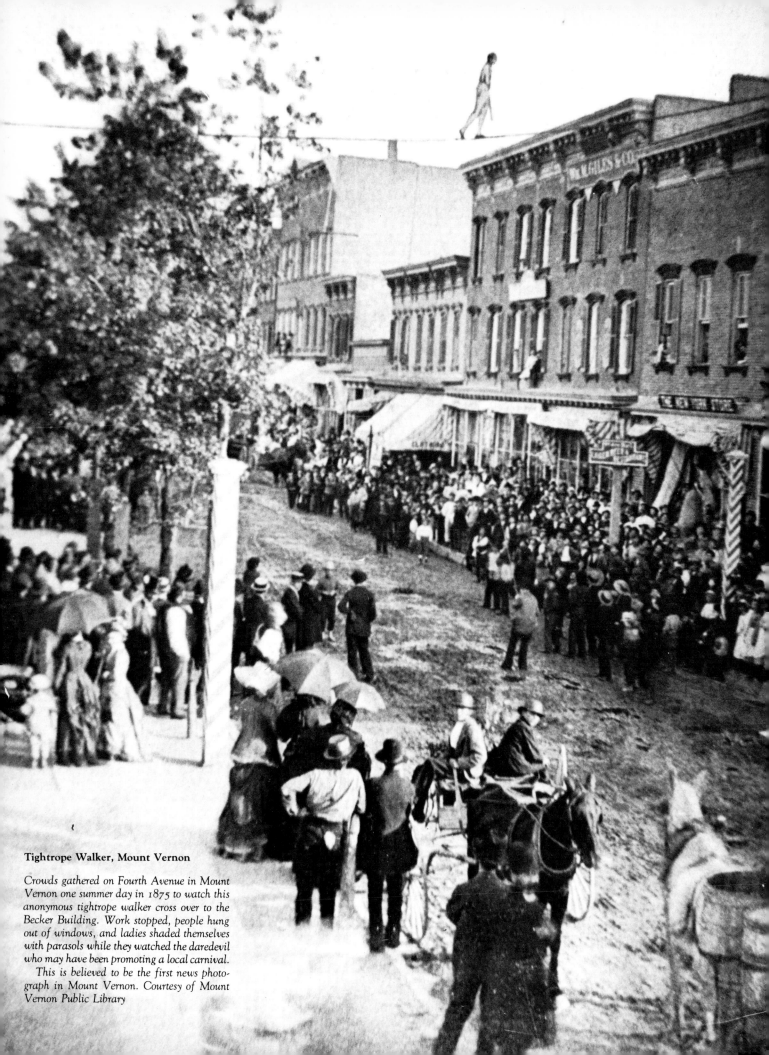

Tightrope Walker, Mount Vernon

Crowds gathered on Fourth Avenue in Mount Vernon one summer day in 1875 to watch this anonymous tightrope walker cross over to the Becker Building. Work stopped, people hung out of windows, and ladies shaded themselves with parasols while they watched the daredevil who may have been promoting a local carnival.

This is believed to be the first news photograph in Mount Vernon. Courtesy of Mount Vernon Public Library

Lancaster O. Underhill

The New York and Harlem Railroad from New York City to White Plains was completed by 1844. Lancaster O. Underhill offered his new home, at Sagamore and Pondfield roads in Bronxville, as a railroad station. Mr. Underhill, shown here relaxing on his porch in the late 1890s, served as both stationmaster and postmaster for fifty years. He died in 1898 at the age of eighty-nine. Courtesy of Westchester County Historical Society

Bronxville Railroad Station

The station in Mr. Underhill's home was known for a time as Underhill's Crossing. There were separate waiting rooms for men and women. The men's waiting room was equipped with a large pot-bellied stove, which stood in a sandpit, also used by tobacco chewers as a spittoon.

After Mr. Underhill's death in 1898 the station was torn down. The present Bronxville station is located near the site. Courtesy of Westchester County Historical Society

Artists' Colony, Bronxville

William Van Duzer Lawrence bought eighty-six acres of farmland in the village of Bronxville in 1890. William A. Bates, a New York architect, was commissioned to design large shingle and stone homes graciously set among the trees and rocks of the former Prescott farm. A narrow, winding, yellow-brick road, laid out by Mr. Lawrence to follow the cow paths, added charm to the landscape which soon attracted many buyers. Bronxville became one of Westchester's most cultured communities, especially noted for its artists and writers. Its art colony peaked before World War I and included painters William H. Howe, T. Herman Schladermundt, and Otto Bacher, among others. In this photograph, taken in 1967, artist Armand Catenaro paints the famous Will Hickok Law studio in the former art colony. Courtesy of Bronxville Public Library

Hotel Gramatan, Bronxville

William Lawrence built the Gramatan Inn, a small colonial inn for fifty guests, in Bronxville in 1897. It burned in 1900.

Five years later Lawrence opened the grand Hotel Gramatan on Sunset Hill. This imposing complex, in the late romantic Spanish-Revival style, contained a ballroom, five dining rooms, and accommodations for 400 guests. A casino, located near today's Garden Avenue, offered tennis courts and bowling alleys and provided hotel guests the opportunity to mingle with local artists and authors who belonged to the Gramatan Country Club, which was also headquartered there. Courtesy of Eastchester Historical Society

Gramatan Arcade, Bronxville

Below the Gramatan nestled the Lawrence Arcade with shops, art studios, and bachelor apartments on the second floor.

The Architectural Record of September 1904 praised the Spanish design of the arcade and hotel, stating, "The many angles of its skyline, from every point of view produce a pleasing effect."

Today a portion of the Lawrence Arcade is all that remains of the Hotel Gramatan complex. The Gramatan Hotel was closed in 1972 and condominiums have been built on the site. Photograph by John Kennedy

Carpenter House, Mount Kisco

This elegant Victorian house, which graces a hilltop on Main Street overlooking the center of Mount Kisco, is typical of the many comfortable homes built in Westchester communities in the years following the Civil War. Mr. Theodore Carpenter, original owner of the house, was prominent in Mount Kisco public affairs, as town assessor, board of education member, and village trustee.

His house, now owned by the Dennis Berger family, was the main setting used in the filming of the movie Ragtime. The Bergers, who had just purchased the house, agreed to delay moving in for several months while the film crews redecorated the interior, landscaped the grounds, and did their shooting. By the time the camera crew was through filming, some of the grandeur had been destroyed—bushes uprooted, grass trampled, and wallpaper burnt by the strong lights. The film crews left, the Bergers moved in, and their lives returned to normal. Courtesy of Mr. and Mrs. Dennis Berger

Carpenter House Dining Room

The dining room in the Carpenter house is shown here as it was decorated for Ragtime. The room was changed after the filming was completed, but the draperies remain. Courtesy of Mr. and Mrs. Dennis Berger

Carpenter House Kitchen

The Carpenter house kitchen was constructed by the Ragtime production crew as a typical kitchen of the early 1900s. Courtesy of Mr. and Mrs. Dennis Berger

Depot School, Mamaroneck

Between 1900 and 1914 Westchester's developing communities began to take on much of the appearance we recognize today. Town services were begun, schools were built, and businesses were established to serve the growing population.

The Depot School in Mamaroneck, on Mamaroneck Avenue and Mount Pleasant Avenue, was built in 1855. When the school population increased, a second story was added. The children shown here had four teachers and a very different educational experience from the children in the one-room schools in the rural section of the county.

The Depot School closed in 1889 when an even larger school was needed. The building was used as a kindergarten until it was demolished in 1927. The school bell is now used at St. Vito's Church. A branch of the Chase Manhattan Bank now occupies the former site of the Depot School. Courtesy of Mamaroneck Historical Society

Dobbs Ferry School Children

In the early twentieth century many more public schools were built to educate the children of the families moving into Westchester. This class of young cooks in Dobbs Ferry evidently enjoyed eating the fruits of their labors. Courtesy of Dobbs Ferry Historical Society

Westchester County National Bank, Peekskill

The bigger towns required more services of all kinds. The Westchester County National Bank of Peekskill is the oldest bank in Westchester. Pierre Van Cortlandt served as its first president when the bank opened for business in 1833.

The bank building, located on the corner of North Division and Main streets, had a house for the cashier next to it, with direct access to the bank as a security measure. In 1955 the Westchester County National Bank merged with the National Bank of Westchester and is now a division of Lincoln First Bank, N. A. It still occupies the original bank building. Courtesy of Westchester County Historical Society

Mamaroneck Bank Interior

Mr. R. G. Brewer serves a customer, possibly a local trolley car conductor, in the Mamaroneck bank in 1894. At this time these offices were shared by both the Union Savings Bank and the First National Bank of Mamaroneck. Courtesy of Mamaroneck Historical Society

Bruechne Barber Shop, New Rochelle

The Bruechne Barber Shop, located at 30 Mechanic Street in New Rochelle, provided one of life's greatest pleasures for gentlemen, a hot shave. In this picture, taken about 1910, a customer reclines in comfort in the oak and velvet chair, his face lathered, and his head resting on a fringed towel, waiting for the barber to take the first scrape with his poised straight razor.

The barber shop was demolished along with other buildings when Mechanic Street was widened and renamed Memorial Highway in the 1970s. Courtesy of Huguenot-Thomas Paine Historical Association, New Rochelle

113

Morton's General Store, Croton-on-Hudson

Morton's General Store, located at the corner of Brook Street and Riverside Avenue in Croton, was established in 1871 by William Morton, Jr. His son Arthur became the first mayor of the village.

This photograph, taken in 1900, shows the wide variety of merchandise available in general stores of the period. Baskets (perhaps made in Dantown), straw hats, pickles, cider, and much more tempted the customer standing at the counter with his shopping basket over his arm. Advertisements hung from the ceiling, illuminated by naked light bulbs.

Morton's General Store was demolished in recent years to make way for construction along Route 9. Courtesy of Historical Reference Room, Croton-On-Hudson Public Library

Ice Wagon, Mamaroneck

The Goodliffe Ice Company's wagon was a familiar sight in Mamaroneck between 1865 and 1920. In this period Mamaroneck Avenue was still paved with cobblestones. The "Danger, Keep Off" sign warned adventurous boys against attempting to hitch rides on the horse-drawn wagon. Courtesy of Mamaroneck Historical Society

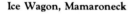

Haguer Building Fire, White Plains

Fire company teamwork extinquished this 1908 fire in the Haguer Building on Main Street in White Plains.

Tragic fires demonstrated the need to bring water into the community for adequate fire protection. Raising taxes for this purpose was the main reason many Westchester communities incorporated in the 1880s and 1890s.

The site of the Haguer Building is now part of the extensive property occupied by the Galleria. Courtesy of White Plains Public Library/Renoda Hoffman

Juvenile Hose Company, Pelham

The Juvenile Hose Company of the Liberty Engine and Hose Company No. 1 in Pelham was composed of boys from the Wartburg Orphanage in nearby Mount Vernon. In this picture the boys, wearing their red uniforms, stand ready to pull the decorated two-wheel hose jumper in the annual Inspection Parade of October 1909.

The Liberty Engine and Hose Company No. 1 was incorporated in 1892 and still fights Pelham's fires from this location on Fifth Avenue. There are two new firehouses, however, in addition to the one pictured here. Courtesy of Pelham Historical Society

Paving Sidewalks, Mamaroneck

Mamaroneck was incorporated in 1896. Public-spirited citizens like Daniel Warren, president of the village from 1902 to 1911, oversaw the installation of streetlights, the paving of the main roads, and other town improvements. Many of the laborers on these work crews were recent immigrants from Italy who settled in Westchester towns.

This view shows the sidewalks being installed on Mamaroneck in the early 1900s. Courtesy of Mamaroneck Historical Society

Trolley on Main Street, Ossining

Horse-drawn trolleys were still operating in lower Westchester in the 1880s. By the end of the decade they were virtually all electrified. One could travel from West Farms (now in the Bronx) through Mount Vernon, Pelham, New Rochelle, and Larchmont for only five cents. By 1903 the Westchester Electric Company had extended its lines to Bronxville, Tuckahoe, Scarsdale, and White Plains.

The Hudson River and Eastern Traction Company operated the trolleys in Ossining until buses replaced them in 1924. This photograph shows a trolley on Main Street about 1905. In the winter the sides of the trolleys were closed and the cars heated by pot-bellied stoves. Courtesy of Ossining Historical Society

Barlow Block, Ossining

The Main Street area of Ossining was restored to its turn-of-the-century appearance in the 1970s. This view of the Barlow Block would have been very familiar to the trolley passengers in the preceding photograph. Photograph from Sanchis, American Architecture: Westchester County

Skippers of the Toonerville Trolley, Pelham

Perhaps no trolley was more famous than the Pelham car immortalized by Fontaine Fox in his syndicated cartoon, "Toonerville Trolley," published from about 1910 until 1955.

Pelham's trolley was one of the small "dinkies" which operated on branch lines in Westchester villages. It ran between Pelham (Shore) Road at the Sound, along Pelhamdale Avenue and Wolf's Lane to the railroad station. Fox got the idea for his cartoon series after riding the already dilapidated trolley to visit a cartoonist friend in 1910. As he recalled in 1921:

> *On the way out the "Skipper" talked with everyone on the car, woke one man up when he got to his usual stop and . . . when I asked if he knew where Charles Voight lived, stopped the car, and led me to the house himself. . . . I thought such a character would lend himself to cartooning.*

In this photograph of the 1920s Pelham skippers Louie and Dan stand proudly in front of their trolley car. Courtesy of Pelham Historical Society

The "Toonerville Trolley"

Cartoonist Fontaine Fox relates how the famous cartoon series was inspired by a visit to Pelham in 1910, and a ride on the Pelham Manor trolley car.

The real Pelham trolley jumped the tracks on many occasions, lending credibility to this cartoon.

"Quite frequently the 'Toonerville' would go coasting on an expedition of its own and leave the rails at the Shore Road end of the line and crack up against the huge boulder on the New York Athletic Club property. The club actually erected a warning signal to remind Skippers of the car that the rock was harder than their battle-scarred vehicles." (Pelham Sun, August 7, 1931).

Skipper Louie took care of his passengers, even waiting for them outside the Pelham Picture House. In fact, the movie house managers had to keep the theater's doors closed on hot summer evenings because the pictures of one movie star in particular always seemed to delay transportation on the "Toonerville." Courtesy of Pelham Historical Society

Steamboat Crystenah, Peekskill

Steamboats plied Long Island Sound and the Hudson River for over 100 years. Their peak of activity was in the late 1800s. Peekskill was one of the major ports on the Hudson River, and the Crystenah was a well-known steamer carrying passengers and freight between Peekskill and New York City. Built in 1869, the Crystenah was wrecked in a gale near New Rochelle in the early 1900s. Courtesy of Westchester County Historical Society

Tarrytown Lighthouse

Sail and steamboat traffic along the Hudson made the need for a lighthouse near Tarrytown apparent as early as the 1840s, but disagreement over its exact location delayed completion until 1883. There had been no real disasters on the river, but unmarked shoals and sandbars presented a potential hazard to shipping. Captain Jacob Ackerman, born in Rockland County and for twenty years a Hudson River skipper, became the lighthouse keeper. He served for twenty-one years and is credited with rescuing nineteen people before his retirement in 1904.

Several other lighthouse keepers succeeded Captain Ackerman, and in 1954 the United States Coast Guard took over the manning of the lighthouse. In 1965 it was decommissioned since navigational lights on the Tappan Zee Bridge made a lighthouse unnecessary.

In 1969 the Westchester County Board of Supervisors acquired the lighthouse for the county to be used for educational programs on the history and ecology of the Hudson River. Courtesy of Historical Society of the Tarrytowns

Mamaroneck Dock

This busy scene was photographed at Mamaroneck Dock about 1898. Passengers are crossing the deck of the Irene Elaine Davis to board the Syosset for a trip to New York City. Note the fish trap on the deck of the small workboat in the foreground. Courtesy of Mamaroneck Historical Society

Traditional Clambake, Mamaroneck

Westchester residents enjoyed many forms of recreation and entertainment in the late 1800s and early 1900s. What could be more mouth-watering than the aroma of fresh-baked clams? The gentleman in the boater waits as the damp sails are lifted from the steaming seaweed covering the clams in the pit. The boys seated in the rear patiently wait to be served at this traditional clambake near the town dock in Mamaroneck in the early 1900s. Courtesy of Mamaroneck Historical Society

Outing of the Chappaqua Shoe Factory, Rye Lake, North Castle

Employees of the Chappaqua Shoe Factory enjoyed a two-week company camping trip to the shores of Rye Lake in North Castle about 1910. Rye Lake later became part of the Kensico Reservoir in 1917, at the completion of the Kensico Dam in Valhalla. Courtesy of Chappaqua Historical Society

Picnic at Rye Lake, Rye

Rye Lake was a popular summer recreational area during this period. Here, Mrs. Hannah Mulhulland, seated at the right in a polka-dotted dress, operated the popular Cliff House guest cottages in Rye. Here she is joined by friends for a sumptuous picnic at the lake. The gentleman holding the knife is William L. Hall. Seated, left to right, are: Sue Mulhulland, Isabelle Hall, and Jennie Garde. The other guests are unidentified. Courtesy of Westchester County Historical Society

Swimming at Oakland Beach, Rye

While the wealthy belonged to exclusive yacht clubs along Long Island Sound, less affluent citizens also enjoyed summer outings on the water.

This family enjoyed swimming at Oakland Beach in Rye in July 1914. The town of Rye had issued bonds to purchase land for the waterfront park at the urging of the townspeople, who were afraid the natural sand beach would be developed into another Coney Island.

Rye Beach is still a popular swimming area for local residents. Courtesy of William Emerick, Ardsley Historian

Glen Island, New Rochelle

Between 1885 and 1914 Glen Island was one of the most extravagant amusement parks in the world. It was developed by John Starin of Rye, who ran a fleet of steamboats from New York to his resort.

By 1891, 20,000 people a day visited Glen Island, which was in fact five islands connected by wooden bridges. The main island had a 4,000-seat Grand Pavilion (now the site of Glen Island Casino), amusement parks, museums, greenhouses, and a zoo. A six-story Japanese pagoda graced another island. Kleine Deutchland ("Little Germany") featured yodelers singing from the towers to attract visitors to the beer garden. There were a dozen bands playing in various locations. At the beach, bathhouses were built to accommodate 800 people.

In 1891 Starin refused an offer of $1.5 million for his fabulous resort, but after World War I the park declined. Westchester County bought Glen Island in 1925, filled in the land between the islands, and combined them into one. A bridge was built to connect the island to the mainland. Glen Island is now operated by the Westchester County Department of Parks, Recreation and Conservation. *Courtesy of Huguenot-Thomas Paine Historical Association, New Rochelle*

121

Bicycle Race, Yonkers

Bicycling became very popular in the 1880s both as a sport and as recreation. This group posed on September 15, 1888, just before the Four Mile Road Race was run in Yonkers.

Bicycles of this type were called ordinaries. Some had front wheels over five feet high, and the racing models pictured here could travel up to twenty miles an hour.

Note at the left of the photograph the unusual bicycle-built-for-two on which the young lady sits as a passenger. Courtesy of the Hudson River Museum, Yonkers

Bicycle Shop, Ossining

By 1895 the new "safety," or familiar low bicycle, had completely replaced the old high-wheeled ordinary.

The dapper young man in the checkered waistcoat is perhaps discussing the purchase of the bicycle-built-for-two standing at the curb. Note the beautifully hand-crafted Rochester Bicycles shipping crate on the sidewalk. *Courtesy of Ossining Historical Society*

Baseball Game, Ossining

Baseball was already established as the national sport in the early 1900s when the Ossining baseball team, pictured here, hosted Pleasantville. There were no benches for the spectators and no backstop for the players, but the crowd looked intently toward third base as the batter in his quilted parts waited for the pitch to drive in a run.

Note the catcher's stance and his crude glove, mask, and pads. The black suits of modern umpires evolved from elegant vested suits like the one worn here. *Courtesy of John Crandall, Pleasantville Historian*

124

Yonkers Canoe Club

Around the turn of the century, canoe clubs were very popular along the Hudson. Here two members of the Yonkers Canoe Club engage in conversation as the canoe Isabel prepares for a ride on the river. Note the jaunty tam-o'-shanter and knickers worn by the gentleman standing on the dock. Courtesy of Hudson River Museum, Yonkers

Ice boating and Driving on the Hudson River at Tarrytown

St. Andrew's Golf Club, Yonkers

This is the first photograph of the game of golf in the United States. It was taken about November 1888 at the original course of the St. Andrew's Golf Club, located on the corner of North Broadway and Shonnard Place in Yonkers.

St. Andrew's Golf Club, organized in the fall of 1888, is the second-oldest existing golf club in the country. Named for the Royal and Ancient Golf Club of St. Andrew's, Scotland, the club was founded by Robert Lockwood, a Scot, who introduced the game to his friends, John B. Upham and John Reid, on February 22, 1888. Both gentlemen are pictured in the photograph which shows (left to right): Harry Holbrook; Warren and Frederick Holbrook, the young caddies; A. P. W. Kinnan; John Upham; and John Reid. Members of the club, located on Jackson Avenue in Hastings since 1897, were instrumental in organizing the U.S. Golf Association. Photograph from St. Andrew's Golf Club, 1888-1938

The frozen Hudson was a popular spot for winter sports up until World War I. Coast Guard cutters did not use icebreakers to keep the channel open until about 1920, and the river often froze over completely for weeks at a time.

This photograph, taken about 1910, shows the old sport of ice boating next to a newer form of excitement, running an automobile on ice. It was considered great fun to get a car going on the ice, slam on the brakes, and see how many corkscrew spins one could make.

Family fun on the frozen Hudson included skating, walking, or driving across the river to Nyack. In an article in the January 31, 1982 Tarrytown Daily News, Katherine Randall of Irvington recalled driving across the river on the ice:

"It was quite hard to get across at first (because of the bumpy ice). Once the first car made a path everyone would follow."

Sometimes autos and horse-drawn carts raced each other or chased freight trains like the one in the background. Courtesy of Historical Society of the Tarrytowns

Tennis at Philipse Manor Country Club, North Tarrytown

A game of mixed doubles was in progress on the tennis court at the Philipse Manor Country Club when this photograph was taken about 1912. The ladies' long skirts kept the game rather slow and sedate, while the dog perhaps served as an automatic ball return.

Philipse Manor Country Club was located on the former Kingsland estate on the Hudson shore in North Tarrytown. An amusement park had been planned for the area, but, instead, an eighty-five-acre public park was developed with a beach, ballfield, picnic grove, and pavilion.

Today, Kingsland Point Park is located on the former country club grounds. It is owned by Westchester County and operated by the Department of Parks, Recreation and Conservation. Courtesy of Westchester County Historical Society

Bobsledding in Briarcliff Manor

Bobsledding was as popular in the early 1900s as it is today. This brave group is coming down Central Drive in Briarcliff Manor. Courtesy of Briarcliff Manor/Scarborough Historical Society

Hudson-Fulton Celebration, Tarrytown

Nineteen nine was the centennial of the first voyage of Robert Fulton's steamboat Clermont up the Hudson River. It was also the tricentennial of Henry Hudson's discovery of the river. The combined Hudson-Fulton Anniversary in September 1909 was one of the largest historical celebrations ever held in this area. Its success reflected the county's growth and prosperity.

Towns all along the Hudson held parades and fireworks displays. In this photograph, taken September 27, spectators watched as 1,542 ships participated in a naval parade that included replicas of the Clermont and the Half Moon, the navy's entire Atlantic fleet, and ships from many other nations. Courtesy of Historical Society of the Tarrytowns

Hudson-Fulton Parade, Briarcliff Manor

Kaiser Wilhelm's son, Crown Prince Wilhelm, was a guest at Briarcliff Lodge in Briarcliff Manor for the Hudson-Fulton festivities. He led a Prussian regiment in the spectacular parade of fifty floats, Indian tribes, U. S. Coast Guard and Signal Corps units, and marching units of British and French marines and sailors held in honor of the celebration in New York.

That evening, Prince Wilhelm and 300 Prussian officers were among the 600 guests who enjoyed a formal dinner given by Howard Carroll at his castle, Carrollcliff, in Tarrytown. Courtesy of Briarcliff Manor/Scarborough Historical Society

Music Hall, Tarrytown

American Yacht Club, Rye

Many of the men who made fortunes in the late 1800s turned to Long Island Sound for sporting recreation. The American Yacht Club was founded in 1882 by financier Jay Gould and several of his friends who owned steam-powered yachts. They built the elegant clubhouse pictured here on Milton Point in Rye.

As the wealthy began to pursue the sport of racing ocean-going sailboats, the American Yacht Club sponsored regattas, races, and elegant parties. Cannon-salutes, full naval welcomes, and tally-ho fanfares for the club's own stage were among the club's rituals.

This building burned in 1951 and has been replaced by a new clubhouse on the same site. Courtesy of Rye Free Reading Room

The Tarrytown Music Hall is Westchester's oldest theater. It was built in 1885 by William L. Wallace, a local chocolate manufacturer. The floor was flat until the 1920s, making possible a wide variety of activities. Roller skating was in vogue between 1880 and 1900, and the Music Hall, along with other theaters in other Westchester communities, was the scene for regular skating parties. The Horticultural Society of the Tarrytowns held annual flower shows at the Music Hall primarily to display the flowers grown on the millionaires' estates along the Hudson.

Motion pictures began to be shown at the Music Hall in 1901. In 1915 the ladies of the Tarrytown Equal Franchise Association held a Cotton Ball to support the cause of women's suffrage, and more than 1,200 people danced to the melodies of Madame Wilson's orchestra.

The Music Hall fell on hard times in recent years but is now the focus of a local effort to restore it for use as a cultural center for performing arts. Courtesy of Historical Society of the Tarrytowns

Regatta Day, Larchmont, N.Y.

Larchmont Yacht Club was founded in 1880 and in 1888 moved into its present clubhouse, the former residence of the railroad executive Benjamin Carver. The establishment of the yacht club went hand-in-hand with the development of Larchmont Manor in the town of Mamaroneck in the 1880s.

Real estate magnate Thompson J. S. Flint bought the fifty-acre Edward Collins estate in 1865 and established the Larchmont Manor Company in 1872. To develop the property as an inducement to buyers, a pleasant park was built along Long Island Sound and a horse trolley line built from the railroad station to the manor. But the greatest impetus to the growth of Larchmont Manor was the suggestion of Flint's son, Frederick, that a yacht club be founded there.

Founding members included Andrew Carnegie, J. P. Morgan, and William K. Vanderbilt. The fashionable activities of this club are seen in the illustration (top) from Harper's Weekly in the 1890s entitled Opening of the Season at Larchmont Yacht Club, New York. The Regatta Day photograph (middle) shows the splendid yachts in the harbor. Race Week (bottom) which is still held at Larchmont Yacht Club, attracts young sailors from all over the East Coast for a week of racing and entertainment. Courtesy of Sydney Astle

Race Week at Larchmont Yacht Club. Larchmont, N.Y.

Four Couples Pose in Front of the Royal Victoria Hotel, Larchmont

This elegant group, perhaps members of a wedding party, posed in front of the Royal Victoria Hotel in Larchmont in the early 1890s. The ladies cannot be identified, but their escorts are (left to right): Charles Perrin, Louis Spencer, Harold Hayward, and Thompson S. Flint.

The Royal Victoria Hotel, located at 20-40 Park Avenue, had a colorful history. It was established in 1895 by Mrs. May C. Wilcox, who had owned two hotels on Forty-second Street in New York and had managed the Turtle Club in Larchmont Park in 1894. Mrs.

Wilcox built the Royal Victoria so quickly that many people said the enormous hotel "had appeared as suddenly as a mushroom—some said a toadstool—one spring day" (Judith Doolan Spikes, "The Way We Were," The Daily Times, July 6, 1981).

The Royal Victoria catered to big-city politicians, theater people, public figures, and affluent tourists. But as the champagne flowed and the sounds of loud music and laughter floated over Larchmont Park, the community rose up in arms. Frederick Flint vainly tried to shut the hotel because its barroom violated the

deed restrictions of the Larchmont Manor Company. Another suit, claiming the hotel was a public nuisance, referred to a "patroness of the hotel bar that had been seen to elevate her skirt to the indecent and scandalous heights of her shoe tops" (Westchester Realty Board, Westchester, August 1935). Mrs. Wilcox prevailed and continued to run the Royal Victoria until her death in 1930.

The hotel has since been torn down, and two modern houses now occupy the site. Courtesy of Westchester Historical Society

Turn-of-the-Century Bride, Mamaroneck

A bride from a well-to-do family in Mamaroneck posed in the hallway of her home before her wedding at the turn of the century. Courtesy of Mamaroneck Historical Society

Gouraud Cottage, Larchmont

Many members of the Larchmont Yacht Club built summer cottages in Larchmont Manor. A typical example was the Amy Crocker Gouraud cottage, built in the 1880s on Oak Bluff Avenue.

Some of the cottages were later converted into boardinghouses and family hotels like the Bevan House. Several well-known actresses of the day who enjoyed vacationing in Larchmont Manor included Louisa Drew (grandmother of John and Ethel Barrymore), Kate Claxton, and Mary Pickford.

Larchmont Manor was a family summer community which was anxious to retain its quiet atmosphere. On one occasion, when news came that undesirable excursionists from Glen Island Park were arriving by train, a greeting party carrying shotguns met them at the Larchmont railroad station and suggested that the visitors return to New Rochelle.

The appeal of living in such pleasant surroundings near the commuter lines soon spurred most owners to winterize their cottages, and Larchmont Manor became a year-round community.

The Gouraud cottage burned in 1904; today the site is occupied by the Larchmont Shore Club. Courtesy of Larchmont Public Library

Dr. Zimmerman in his Reo, Pleasantville

The coming of the automobile in the early 1900s had a profound effect on Westchester County. Dr. Zimmerman of Pleasantville is shown in this photograph, taken about 1905, sitting proudly in his Reo automobile. Doctors were among the first to make practical use of the automobile, bouncing along unpaved roads to make their house calls. Courtesy of John Crandall, Pleasantville Historian

Dobbs Ferry-Hastings Auto Club

Automobile clubs, such as the Dobbs Ferry-Hastings Auto Club pictured here, sprang up in Westchester County in the early 1900s. This photograph was taken when the club gathered for a Saturday outing about 1910.

Recreational driving was fun for the entire family as the children in dusters and goggles illustrate. Often as many as fifteen or twenty cars would travel together. Choking in each other's dust, the group would ride along country roads to some pre-arranged location. Then out would come the big picnic baskets, and the members would enjoy an afternoon of relaxation and games before heading home. Photograph from Life of a River Village: Dobbs Ferry

Judge Raven's Cider Stand, Armonk

Residents in northern Westchester soon realized that automobile clubs and other weekend drivers loved to bring home souvenirs from their trips to the country. Cider stands, like the one belonging to Judge Raven in Armonk, popped up along the country roads. Here the judge can be seen in his cap, selling apples, cider, and pumpkins.

Seventy-five years later, families still take pleasure in driving to this area to bring home a Halloween pumpkin and fresh apples for applesauce and pies. Courtesy of North Castle Historical Society

Port of Missing Men, North Salem

The Port of Missing Men, a tea house named after a popular novel of the time, was built in 1907. Between 1908 and 1910 it attracted over 20,000 people to its remote location on a high hill in North Salem. Visitors enjoyed the food and the view of the far hills from the tearoom's glassed porches.

Many of the visitors came to investigate buying property and building homes in the area near the tea house developed by Henry B. Anderson. Mr. Anderson and his associates had bought about forty farms on the Connecticut border of Westchester County. They built ten miles of roads and brought in water and sewers. Lakes were dug and building lots set out. The tea house looked over these beautiful properties offered for sale.

The development, which Mr. Anderson hoped would rival Tuxedo Park, never came to fruition. World War I ended the sales promotion, and Mr. Anderson departed for Long Island. The tea house continued to operate into the 1930s but was finally sold to a developer in 1956. It now belongs to Westchester County and is the site of Mountain Lakes Camp, operated by the Department of Parks, Recreation and Conservation. *Courtesy of Westchester County Historical Society*

Florence Inn, Tarrytown

Florence Inn, located on the corner of Franklin Street and Broadway in Tarrytown, is shown here decorated for a Fourth of July parade in 1917. Attractive hanging baskets of ferns line the veranda, set with tables for guests. The inn's sign, which advertised "Good Food and Good Service," was borne out by its reputation, and the inn was a popular spot for travelers along Broadway.

The inn was opened in 1821 as the Franklin House and was a stagecoach stop on the old Albany Post Road (now Broadway, Route 9.) It was also known as Vincent House before it became the Florence Inn. Washington Irving frequently dined here, and other distinguished visitors included four presidents: Martin Van Buren, Rutherford B. Hayes, Theodore Roosevelt, and Woodrow Wilson.

The Florence Inn prospered until World War II. It was torn down in 1964, and the site is now occupied by the Metropolitan Life Insurance Company. *Courtesy of Historical Society of the Tarrytowns*

On April 24, 1908, the American International Race for Stock Cars, commonly known as the Briarcliff Stock Car Race, was run for the Briarcliff trophy and $10,000 offered by Walter Law of Briarcliff Manor.

Twenty-two entrants raced seven times around the thirty-five-mile course which ran from Briarcliff to Kitchawan, and thence through Mount Kisco, Armonk, Kensico, Eastview, and back to Briarcliff. This was a distance of 240 miles over treacherous dirt roads. Over 300,000 people watched the race along its route, thousands of whom walked from White Plains to viewing spots at Eastview and Kensico. Hundreds of bonfires took the chill out of the April night in the hours before the race, and "there was not a frankfurter to be purchased in any store" Frank MacNicol

Briarcliff Stock Car Race, Briarcliff Manor

recalled forty-two years later for the White Plains Reporter Dispatch.

People along the roads waited expectantly for the first racer to come in sight. Finally, "down the road in a cloud of dust came one of the roaring monsters. In a flash it was by, and it was the daring Italian, Cedrino. Then came Danny Murphy, and a roar from the crowd, for Danny was driving like mad and the hopes of Westchester rooters ran high. (Danny was from White Plains)...(Barney) Olfield, with the famous cigar in his mouth, was not used to following anyone and came in for a lot of good-natured joshing from the crowd."

The race was won by Louis Strang, driving an Italian-made Isotta-Franschini, in five hours, fourteen minutes, and thirteen seconds. Courtesy of Westchester County Historical Society

The crowd watching the Briarcliff Stock Car Race was stunned when news came back that Danny Murphy had gone out of the race in the fourth lap. The spokes broke in his right front wheel, breaking his front axle and landing him in a ditch.

This photograph, taken in Armonk, may have been Murphy's wreck or that of a contestant named DePalma, driving an Allen-Kingston, who also ended the race in a ditch. Surprisingly, these were the only two cars wrecked. *Courtesy of North Castle Historical Society*

Car Wreck Near Armonk During the Briarclfff Stock Car Race

View of Hastings, by Jasper Francis Cropsey

Jasper Francis Cropsey, painter of this autumn scene in Hastings, was born in 1823 on Staten Island. He originally trained as an architect and took up painting so he could put landscape backgrounds into his architectural drawings.

He enjoyed such success at painting that in 1866 he built a large home and studio in Warwick, New York. In 1885 Cropsey sold his Warwick home and moved to Hastings. He added a studio onto his house there and continued to paint until his death in 1900. The

house has since been occupied by the Cropsey family and their descendants. Located at 49 Washington Avenue in Hastings-on-Hudson, it is now maintained by the Newington-Cropsey Foundation as a museum.

The painting shown here was executed in 1893. At the far left can be seen the square roof of Cropsey's studio. The path in the center is the Aqueduct Road, and the small house in the foreground still stands. *Courtesy of Newington-Cropsey Foundation, Hastings*

134

Presidential Campaign Picnic for Horace Greeley in Chappaqua

Many well-known people made Westchester their home in the years between the Civil War and World War I. Horace Greeley, editor of the New York Tribune, was the Liberal Republican candidate for president in 1872, running against the regular Republican candidate, the incumbent Ulysses S. Grant.

Greeley, advocating amnesty for the South, also received the nomination of the Democrats when they concluded that a coalition offered the only possible opportunity for winning the election.

At the beginning of the campaign, a picnic for Democratic delegates was held in the evergreen grove on Greeley's farm in Chappaqua. Trainloads of guests arrived to enjoy a lavish buffet and to hear campaign speeches. In this wood engraving, Greeley can be seen greeting delegates under the sign reading "No Smoking in this Grove." No liquor was served either, which surprised many of the visitors.

Greeley had owned property in Chappaqua since 1853. He had a seventy-eight-acre farm and a house in the village which still stands on King Street (Route 120). The barn on his farm is now a private home, located on Aldridge Road. The road where the picnic was held is now on the grounds of the Episcopal Church of St. Mary the Virgin on Greeley Avenue. *Courtesy of Chappaqua Historical Society*

Grant Family at Merryweather, North Salem

Greeley's opponent, President Ulysses S. Grant, was also connected to Westchester County. President Grant's son, Ulysses, Jr., married Fannie Chafee, the daughter of Colorado Senator Jerome Chafee, in 1880. Merryweather, the house located at June and Grant roads in North Salem, was Senator Chafee's wedding gift to the young couple.

After he retired from political life, President Grant was a frequent visitor at Merryweather until his death in 1885. Grant enjoyed driving matched Arabian horses along June Road (Route 124) and wrote a large part of his memoirs here.

In this photograph, Grant's daughter-in-law Fannie stands at center behind the former president. Grant's wife is seated on the left and his son on the right.

Merryweather was later occupied by the family of Chafee Grant, the president's grandson. It is still a private residence. Courtesy of Westchester County Historical Society

Elizabeth Custer, the handsome and much-admired widow of General George Custer, built a home in 1892 in Lawrence Park, Bronxville, on Park Avenue next to the home of an old school friend, Mrs. Arthur Wellington.

In 1906 she built a second home nearby, with two towers, large fireplaces, and imposing rooms in which she enjoyed entertaining. Courtesy of Huguenot-Thomas Paine Historical Association, New Rochelle

Elizabeth Custer, Bronxville

The Leatherman

Every locality has its eccentric figures, some feared and others simply wondered at. What caused the Leatherman to pursue such a strange way of life can only be surmised. He is believed to have been a Frenchman named Jules Bourglay, probably born around 1834, who came to America in 1858, some say to escape the pain of a broken heart. He always dressed in a suit of leather patches, and he had no permanent home. Instead, he traveled a long circular route through Connecticut and lower New York State, walking the same roads over and over.

The Leatherman lived through the charity of local housewives, who responded with food and drink to his knock at their doors. Louise Boughton of Lewisboro had this recollection of the strange figure:

> The Leatherman came around once a year. He would always come to the east side of the house. He would never look at you. He would knock on the leader drain pipe. Mother would give him coffee and some sandwiches, or dinner if it was dinnertime. He would say 'Thank you so much, lady,' but never look at you. Sometimes he would stay in the Sarah Bishop cave. He was dressed in brown leather. No one was afraid of him.

The Leatherman's wanderings came to an end in 1889, when he died from a cancer of the mouth which he had suffered from for some time. He is buried in the Sparta Cemetery in Ossining. Courtesy of Westchester County Historical Society

Jimmy-Under-the-Rock

Another well-known Westchester hermit, unlike the Leatherman, had a permanent home. When Jimmy Johnson, at odds with the world even as a boy, quarreled with his family and left home, he soon found the ideal spot to live the solitary life he sought. In a ravine about a half-mile from where Kensico Dam now stands, he found an overhanging rock sticking out twenty feet from the bank. The fifteen-foot-high space beneath this ledge became his one-room house, and he built a wall to close it in, complete with door and windows. Thus he became "Jimmy-Under-the-Rock," and there he stayed.

He kept some farm animals and rode into White Plains on his old white horse once a week for supplies. To protect himself from the copperhead snakes common to the area, he suspended a wagon box from the rock ceiling and used a ladder to get into his makeshift bed. When he was found dead in this bed from pneumonia in 1881, he was believed to have been at least eighty years old. *Courtesy of Westchester County Historical Society*

Madame C. J. Walker, Irvington

America's first black millionairess was Madame C. J. Walker. She was born Sarah Breedlove, in a poor cabin in Louisiana in 1867. She was the daughter of ex-slaves. In 1905 she had a dream which gave her a formula that would stop hair from falling out. She manufactured some of the mixture and was soon selling it door to door among her black neighbors.

The claim that using her formula also straightened hair led her to advertise the preparation. She opened beauty salons and was such a shrewd businesswoman that by 1915 she was worth at least a million dollars.

Her mansion, designed by black architect Vertner Tandy, was named by Enrico Caruso, who took the first two letters of each word in Mrs. Walker's daughter's name, Lelia Walker Robinson, to create the word Lewaro. Located on Broadway (Route 9) in Irvington, it is now the Annie E. Poth Home for "tired mothers, convalescents and the aged," run by the Companions of the Forest in America. *Courtesy of Westchester County Historical Society*

Octagon House, Irvington

The wealthy built many huge mansions and weekend retreats in Westchester between 1865 and 1920. The Octagon House on West Clinton Avenue in Irvington is one of only two domed octagonal houses in the United States; the other is Longwood in Natchez, Mississippi. The Octagon House was built in 1860 by Philip Armour, a wealthy banker who was also a keen student of phrenology, a system of analyzing a person's character by studying bumps on the head. The house was constructed to resemble the human brain. Ten years later, it was bought by Joseph Stiner, the tea merchant, and redecorated as a colorful summer pavilion.

The Octagon House has fifteen large rooms and fifteen small triangular rooms with many triangular closets. The house has had several owners, including historian Carl Carmer.

In 1979 Joseph Pell Lombardi, a restoration architect, bought the house from the National Trust for Historic Preservation. He is restoring the house to its appearance during Stiner's ownership. *Courtesy of Westchester County Historical Society*

Charles Butler, Scarsdale

Charles Butler was born at Kinderhook Landing, New York, in 1802. In 1820 his brother, Benjamin F. Butler, was Martin Van Buren's law partner, and Charles lived in the Van Buren home while serving as a law clerk in the Van Buren firm. Butler eventually went to New York City, where he became a successful lawyer and finacier.

In 1853 Butler began purchasing property in Fox Meadow in Scarsdale, hoping the country air would improve the health of his son Ogden. Butler eventually assembled 491 acres, almost 12 percent of current Scarsdale.

Ogden spent the last three years of his life improving the farm. He planned the gardens and started the greenhouses where he cultivated grapes.

Charles Butler continued to improve Fox Meadow until his death in 1897; he bequeathed the property to his daughter Emily. *Courtesy of Scarsdale Public Library*

Lord and Burnham, Irvington

The Lord and Burnham Greenhouse Manufacturing Company was established in Syracuse, New York, in 1856 and moved to Irvington in 1870 to be nearer to its wealthy clientele along the Hudson River. Its first building burned in 1881, and another was constructed on the same site. The building now houses the administrative offices of the company, which is known as the Burnham Corporation.

This engraving shows the plant as it looked when Hudson River schooners docked at the Burnham pier to load and unload greenhouse materials. The present factory buildings at Irvington were built in 1894, on a site to the south created by filling in the Hudson River. *Courtesy of Irvington Historical Society*

Charles Butler lived the life of a country gentleman on Fox Meadow Estate, which was located between Fenimore Road, Wayside Lane, the Post Road, and the Bronx River. He grew wheat and barley and kept a small herd of cattle. The large greenhouses in the photograph, almost certainly manufactured by Lord and Burnham, supplied flowers for the formal gardens and the house, which faced the Post Road. Much of the property was left in its natural state. Members of the family and their guests greatly enjoyed walking and horseback riding along paths through the woods.

When Emily Butler inherited the property in 1897, she opened the grounds of Fox Meadow to pedestrians and equestrians. She later sold or donated parcels of land for the Bronx River Parkway, Scarsdale High School, and Wayside Inn. In 1925 the remainder of the property was sold to real estate developers who built gracious homes on the former estate. *Courtesy of Scarsdale Public Library*

The Ward Castle in Port Chester was built by William E. Ward, a hardware manufacturer, in 1876. It is believed to be the first residence built entirely of reinforced concrete.

The most famous occupant of Ward Castle was Ward's son, William L. Ward. He was the undisputed leader of the Republican party in Westchester County for almost forty years and is credited with doing more to develop modern Westchester than any other man. During his leadership, the parkway, recreation, health, sewer, zoning, and other systems were established throughout the county. "He felt Westchester was the most wonderful place on earth and did everything he could to make it a finer place to live," stated his obituary in the New York Times in 1933.

Today Ward Castle, located at Comly Avenue and King Street in Port Chester, is the home of the Museum of Cartoon Art. *Photograph by Frank Ledermann*

Ben Holladay, a flamboyant millionaire called America's King of Transportation, built Ophir Hall on Purchase Street in 1864. Holladay lost his fortune in the panic of 1873, and the Purchase property was acquired in 1888 by Whitelaw Reid, owner of the New York Tribune, who extensively remodeled it.

Only a month before the remodeling was completed, the entire mansion was destroyed by fire. Reid hired the architectural firm of McKim, Mead and White to rebuild it. The new Ophir Hall contained a magnificent reception hall with walls of yellow Numidian marble and pink marble from Georgia. Parlor rooms came from a French chateau, and Frederick Law Olmsted, the landscape architect of Central Park, designed the formal gardens. An English wing was later added to the house, which included a huge Tudor-style library.

Whitelaw Reid ran unsuccessfully for vice-president with Benjamin Harrison in 1892 and was later named ambassador to England in 1905. After his death in 1912, his wife

Fox Meadow Estate, Scarsdale

Ward Castle, Port Chester

Ophir Hall, Purchase

Elisabeth, the daughter of D. Ogden Mills, remained active, serving as chairman of the American Red Cross during World War I. Her son, Ogden Reid, merged his newspaper with the Herald to create the New York Herald Tribune. He and his wife Helen lived across the street from his mother in Ophir cottage.

Ophir Hall is today Reid Hall, the administration building of Manhattanville College. *Photograph from Sanchis, American Architecture: Westchester County*

The king of Siam came to the United States for eye surgery in 1931, and at the government's request, Elisabeth Reid generously offered Ophir Hall for the king's stay. King Prajadhipok and his entourage stayed several months at Ophir, and he underwent his cataract surgery in an operating room set up in a large room in the mansion. After his recovery he was the first Oriental monarch to visit the White House. Courtesy of the Charles Dawson History Center, Harrison

The King of Siam at Ophir Hall, Purchase

Lyndhurst, Tarrytown

Lyndhurst, a Gothic Revival mansion on the Hudson River in Tarrytown, was bought by railroad magnate Jay Gould in 1880. It had originally been built in 1838 for General William Paulding by the famous architect Alexander Jackson Davis. In 1864 Davis added the tower and dining room wing for a new owner, George Merritt, who in turn sold it to Gould.

After Jay Gould died in 1892, his daughter Helen lived in the house until her death in 1938. Gould's second daughter Anna, the Dutchess of Tallyrand-Perigord, moved into Lyndhurst in 1939. At her death in 1961, the estate was given to the National Trust for Historic Preservation. Restoration has continued at Lyndhurst since 1964. The mansion is open to the public, and it has been the site of many recreational events, including the summer concerts of the Westchester County Orchestra. Courtesy of Lyndhurst, a Property of the National Trust for Historic Preservtion

Gardening Class at Lyndhurst

The many philanthropies of Helen Gould made her greatly beloved in the community. She earned a Congressional Gold Medal for her devoted service to the sick and wounded during the Spanish-American War. She often opened her home to the children of the area as well as to underprivileged children from New York. She held sewing classes and fresh air parties and taught children how to garden, as seen in this 1905 photograph. Courtesy of Lyndhurst, a Property of the National Trust for Historic Preservation

Helen Gould Shepard and Family

Helen Gould married Finley K. Shepard in 1913. The Shepards decided to adopt a family although adoption was almost unheard of among members of the wealthy upper classes at this time. It was perhaps Mrs. Shepard's most generous act, for by adopting Olivia, shown here walking between her parents, she helped to make adoption fashionable. The Shepards added three other children to the family, Finley J., Helen Anna, and Louis Seton, who shared the luxurious life at Lyndhurst with their parents. Courtesy of Lyndhurst, a Property of the National Trust for Historic Preservation

Rockwood Hall, North Tarrytown

Rockwood Hall, built by William Rockefeller, brother of John D. Rockefeller, Sr., in 1886-87, was the grandest of many grand castles along the Hudson River. It contained 204 rooms and was set on 1,000 acres of beautiful property graced by miles of private roads. Peacocks wandered in gardens groomed by 100 groundskeepers.

When William Rockefeller died in 1922, the property became the Rockwood Hall Country Club, which failed during the Depression.

I. B. M. World Trade Americas/Far East Corporation built its headquarters in 1975 on the property, which is located between Phelps Memorial Hospital and Sleepy Hollow Country Club on Broadway (Route 9) in North Tarrytown. The Rockwood Hall gatehouse still stands at the north entrance to I. B. M. Courtesy of Westchester County Historical Society

Kykuit, Rockefeller Family Home, Pocantico Hills

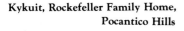

Christmas Tree at Lyndhurst

This magnificent Victorian Christmas tree was decorated at Lyndhurst in the early 1900s for Helen Gould's nieces, Dorothy and Helen. Ordinarily the Goulds closed Lyndhurst for the winter and spent Christmas in New York, but on several occasions, when Helen's brother Frank and his family came to visit, the Christmas holiday was spent at Lyndhurst. Courtesy of Lyndhurst, a Property of the National Trust for Historic Preservation

John D. Rockefeller, Sr., began buying land in Pocantico in 1893. He bought seventeen farms totaling 3,500 acres and built his home, which he called Kykuit ("lookout" in Dutch). This house burned in 1902 and was replaced in 1913 by the present Colonial Revival style home, set in a 300-acre park on top of a hill with a fifty-mile view of the Hudson River.

Over the years, John D., Sr., and his son, John D., Jr., developed the property to include over sixty buildings, an eighteen-hole golf course, a million-dollar recreation facility they called The Playhouse, formal gardens, fountains, and terraces.

John D. Rockefeller, Jr., raised his family on the estate; after his death Kykuit was occupied by his son Nelson, who added a Japanese garden and tea house to hold his collection of sculpture. His brothers, John D. Rockefeller III, Laurance, and David, also maintained homes on the property.

The Rockefellers bought 98 percent of the village of Pocantico Hills outside the park and transformed the hamlet into a unique residential community. All unattractive commercial buildings, such as stores, the railroad station, a hotel, gas stations, and even public phone booths were removed. The village has been occupied primarily by employees on the Rockefeller estate. The Rockefellers generously donated the school, firehouse, and churches to the village. Union Church, which was built by the Rockefellers in 1922, is noted for stained-glass windows by Henri Matisse, donated by the family as a memorial to Abbey Aldrich Rockefeller in 1956, and for a series of Marc Chagall windows, donated as a memorial to John D., Jr., in 1964.

In October 1981 Laurance Rockefeller announced plans to donate 1,500 acres of the 3,500-acre estate for use as a state park. The park will be operated by the Taconic State Park Commission. Kykuit will be operated by Sleepy Hollow Restorations (the non-profit organization established by the Rockefellers to manage their restorations). Courtesy of Rockefeller Archive Center, Pocantico Hills

This charming family portrait was taken about 1916. In the front row, left to right, are: Laurance, John D., Sr. (holding David), Winthrop, Abbey Aldrich Rockefeller, and Nelson. Standing, left to right, are: Abbey, John D., Jr., and John D. III.

The Rockefellers' generosity and philanthropies are legion. John D., Jr., retired from the business world to manage and give away much of the fortune his father had amassed. Rockefeller University, dedicated to medical research, was formed, and the several Rockefeller foundations were established which have contributed millions of dollars to worthy charities. The Rockefeller interest in historic preservation rescued Williamsburg, Virginia, as well as Sunnyside, Philipsburgh Manor, and Van Cortlandt Manor in Westchester County. *Courtesy of Rockefeller Archive Center, Pocantico Hills*

Carrie Chapman Catt, New Rochelle

The women's suffrage movement reached its peak of activity after 1914. Carrie Chapman Catt, pictured here at the age of seventy-seven, was for many years president of the International Alliance for Women's Suffrage. Her home in New Rochelle was a mecca for women's rights advocates.

Mrs. Catt decided to win women the right to vote at the age of twelve, when her father told her the reason her mother couldn't vote was that she "didn't know enough." "Mother knows more than those men," she replied (New York Herald Tribune, January 5, 1936). After the long crusade for women's suffrage was successfully completed in 1920, Mrs. Catt found another cause, the movement for world peace, to which she devoted her time and energies. Courtesy of Westchester County Historical Society

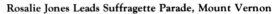

Rosalie Jones Leads Suffragette Parade, Mount Vernon

Rosalie Jones, an internationally-known suffragette leader (left), reins in her steed before leading a parade for women's suffrage in Mount Vernon in 1913.

The Women's Suffrage and Protective Labor Committee had been active in Mount Vernon since September 15, 1868, when Susan B. Anthony spoke at Union Hall on the right of women to vote in local elections. Part of the crowd which packed the hall that evening were members of the board of village trustees, who decided against holding their regular board meeting because it would conflict with Miss Anthony's speech. "The men thought they could do better by attending the women's suffrage meeting" (Village News, September 23, 1868). Courtesy of Mount Vernon Public Library

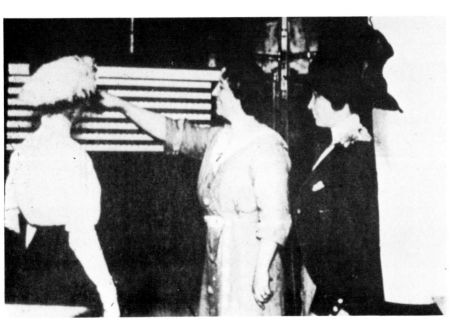

Women Learning How to Use a Voting Booth, Scarsdale

Mrs. Frank Bethell organized the Scarsdale Suffrage League in 1915. Emily Butler was a strong supporter and offered Wayside Cottage as a headquarters for the suffragettes.

In 1916, when the suffrage amendment was defeated at the polls, Mrs. Bethell hung a large yellow placard at Wayside Cottage which told it all: "Victory Postponed. Regular meeting next Tuesday."

It was a proud day when these Scarsdale women gathered at the voting booth to learn how to cast their first ballots. Courtesy of Scarsdale Public Library

Cadillac Eight Recruiting Car, White Plains

When the United States entered World War I, Westchester County men responded overwhelmingly to the call to arms. This Cadillac Eight recruiting car was parked in front of the county courthouse in White Plains in 1917. Courtesy of Westchester County Historical Society

Red Cross Volunteers Rolling Bandages, White Plains

Women joined the American Red Cross to do their part for the boys overseas. This large group of volunteers met in White Plains in 1918 to roll bandages. Courtesy of White Plains Public Library/Renoda Hoffman

Farmerettes, Scarsdale

Some of the women of Scarsdale aided the war effort by organizing a community farm, which operated along Wayside Lane on thirty acres of land donated by Emily Butler. Their plan was to take Scarsdale off the food market as far as winter vegetables were concerned. Boy Scouts helped by clearing the land, and the women did the planting. Shares were sold to raise capital for the venture, and a superintendent was hired and given quarters in Wayside Cottage.

In this photograph the women are looking over the fruits of their labor. Although the farm yielded about 1,350 bushels of vegetables the first season, the venture was a financial loss and was ended. Courtesy of Scarsdale Public Library

146

Home Guard Drilling on the Hudson River, Hastings-on-Hudson

Men who were unable to join the regular army because of age or marital status, often joined Home Defense battalions. This unit, pictured drilling on the frozen Hudson River near Hastings-on-Hudson during the winter of 1917-18, was considered one of the best in New York State. The men usually practiced on their own drill ground, which had a rifle range.

Regular army troops were stationed in Hastings to prevent sabotage in the mustard-gas plant at the Zinsser factory, located at the southern end of Hastings's industrial area. The Paul Ulich Company and Tappan Tanker Company are located on the site today. Courtesy of Hastings-on-Hudson Public Library

Liberty Ball Rolls to Dobbs Ferry

Local Westchester towns rallied behind the drive to buy Liberty Bonds to finance the war. Parades were held in local villages and towns, and people reached deep into their pockets to support the war effort.

Local boys in Dobbs Ferry surrounded the battered Liberty Ball, a huge replica of the world, which was rolled from Buffalo to New York City to raise support for the Liberty Bond drive. Photograph from Dobbs Ferry: Life of a River Village

Chapter 4

1920-1983:

Westchester Comes of Age

Rural life continued in northern Westchester in the 1920s much as it had before World War I. There were many farms still shipping milk, fruit, and vegetables to New York and Connecticut. Small hamlets and villages remained isolated along unpaved roads, and children continued to attend one-room schoolhouses just as their fathers and grandfathers had done. The Depression drove many farmers out of business altogether, and the dairy farms began to break up as competition from other areas lowered the demand for Westchester farm products. Rising land taxes and falling profits led most of the remaining farmers to sell out to real estate developers after World War II. In 1964, 18,500 acres were farmed in Westchester. Ten years later only 9,000 acres were farmed.

South of White Plains, the few remaining farms disappeared rapidly after 1920 as suburbanization began in earnest. Republican party leader William L. Ward influenced the County Board of Supervisors to create the Westchester County Planning Commission and gathered a team of outstanding county citizens to carry out his dream of developing Westchester into a suburban paradise. An overall plan for golf courses, parkways, and recreational areas created a network of beautiful open areas throughout the county.

The Bronx River Parkway was the highway that opened up Westchester. It had been begun in 1906 as part of the project to clean up the Bronx River, which had become a badly contaminated eyesore by the turn of the century. In the process of building the parkway, the Bronx River bed was cleaned and dredged, 30,000 trees and 140,000 shrubs were planted, and paths and benches for the public were set among the trees and lakes. When it opened in 1925 the Bronx River Parkway immediately drew worldwide attention to Westchester County.

The Bronx River Parkway was followed by the Saw Mill River Parkway, the Hutchinson River Parkway, the Taconic Parkway, and the Cross County Parkway, all completed by the 1930s. The scenic beauty of Westchester's parkways is still fresh fifty years later. The next major road construction did not take place until the 1950s and 1960s, when the interstate expressways and thruways were built.

The parkways brought many young, middle-class executives and professionals to Westchester to buy new homes being erected on old estates. The prosperity of the post-war period put cash in the pockets of many young families. They invested in real estate, which rapidly increased in value. Buying a home became the goal of everyone who could afford it.

Transportation was developed to accommodate the growing

Untermeyer Gardens, Yonkers
Courtesy of Hudson River Museum, Yonkers

149

population. Local roads were paved, traffic regulations developed, and traffic lights installed. As the roadways improved, buses replaced the old trolley system. The Toonerville Trolley of Pelham made its last run in 1937; the Westchester bus system had replaced it.

As suburban towns grew, men and women organized a variety of social, cultural, and educational organizations within them. The combination of companionship and worthwhile volunteer service appealed to women like those who had been active in the suffragette movement and World War I relief organizations. Women also nurtured the arts and other cultural activities. Membership in womens' clubs and service organizations became an integral part of the suburban life that emerged in Westchester during the 1920s and continues into the 1980s.

People enjoyed many leisure activities in Westchester during the period between the world wars. Among the achievements of William Ward and the parks commission was the creation of an overall plan for recreational areas in the county. Rye, Playland amusement area opened to acclaim in 1928. Ward Pound Ridge Reservation, Croton Point Park, Glen Island Park, and Kingsland Point Park were also developed by the county for the public. In 1930 the County Center was opened in White Plains as an all-purpose convention space for exhibits and events.

Construction of Cross County Parkway, Pelham
Courtesy of Pelham Historical Society

Armonk Airport was a great recreational attraction in the late 1920s and 1930s. People came from miles around to watch the planes and barnstormers. Roadside stands and the Log Cabin Restaurant catered to the crowds. Residents still recall the phenomenal traffic jams along Bedford Road.

The entertainment industry had a brief moment of glory in Westchester when D. W. Griffith operated his movie studio complex on Orienta Point in Mamaroneck. The Gish sisters, Mary Pickford, and many other famous movie stars of the day were filmed in the Griffith studios and also on location around the county. Legitimate theater also took precarious hold in Westchester soil. The Lawrence family opened the Lawrence Farms Theatre, the first summer-stock theater in Westchester, in a barn on the former Moses Taylor estate in Mount Kisco. Day Tuttle and Richard Skinner leased the barn in 1932, and throughout the 1930s great actors and actresses like Tallulah Bankhead, Henry Fonda, and Margaret Sullivan appeared there.

The Depression hit Westchester as badly as it did the rest of the nation. Communities rallied to provide support for the unemployed. Many of the work projects sponsored by the federal government are still enjoyed by county residents today.

The period between the wars saw a number of new businesses arriving in Westchester. When B. Altman's opened a branch in White Plains in 1934, it was the first major New York department store to come to Westchester. Best and Company, Peck and Peck, and Sloane's followed in the 1940s, and White Plains became the major shopping center in Westchester County. The man credited with this development of "Little Fifth Avenue" was Leonard H. Davidow, who set a high standard of excellence in his dealings.

The *Reader's Digest* developed into a major publishing concern in Pleasantville during the 1930s. When the magazine outgrew its rented office space in Pleasantville, it built a spectacular colonial-style headquarters which still dominates a hill overlooking the Saw Mill River Parkway in Chappaqua.

During World War II the county once again rallied for the war effort. General Motors manufactured airplane parts, Norden bomb sights were made in White Plains, and the Alexander Smith Carpet Mills turned out tents and uniforms for the armed forces. Westchester residents enthusiastically supported scrap-iron drives for Britain in 1940. Then after the bombing of Pearl Harbor in December 1941, they sent their men and boys overseas to join the Allied forces. On the home front men and women worked in the factories, joined the Civil Defense League, watched for enemy planes, and took first aid classes to be prepared in case of an enemy attack. Many took British and French children into their homes. They bought war bonds and endured the inconveniences of food and gas rationing. Then on VJ Day, August 5, 1945, it was over, and Westchester joined the rest of the nation in parades and celebrations of joy.

The post-World War II period of the 1950s was one of prosperity and optimism. Veterans returned home, married, entered the job market, and raised large families. The baby boom was on, and Westchester responded to it by building high-rise apartments, single-family homes, and schools. Ranch houses, split levels, and clapboard and stone colonials filled up the vacant lots in lower Westchester. North of White Plains, developers built hundreds of new homes in the fields and woods of the old farms. "Chappaqua exists today because it contained great areas of open land suitable for housing developments," stated Frances Cook Lee, New Castle Town Historian. Schools were built to accommodate the influx of school-age chldren. A new era of suburbanization had begun.

One of the characteristics of suburban life in the 1950s was its focus on children and the family. A wide range of social, cultural, and sports activities was developed for young people. It seemed as if parents who had endured the Depression as children and the war as young adults wanted their own children to experience a full life. Families barbecued, camped, and played together. Country clubs, which had catered primarily to golf- and tennis-playing adults in earlier years, built swimming pools and offered competitive swimming, diving, and tennis programs for members' children.

Women in the 1950s and 1960s generally preferred to work before their children were born and, if necessary, after they were grown. However, many middle-class women did not need to work and hoped to marry soon after finishing their education. Women continued to spend the majority of their time caring for their homes and children. Social, cultural, and service clubs filled their leisure hours and satisfied their need for companionship during the day.

Since 1960 the arts have received increasing attention from the Westchester community. An educated population offered support and volunteer time to help promote historical and art museums and the performing arts. The Katonah Gallery is an outstanding example of a professional and volunteer staff working closely together to create highly professional art exhibits and programs for the public and for the schools. Many communities have active arts councils as well as private schools of dance, music, and art. In 1965 the Council of the Arts of

St. Andrew's Golf Course, Hastings-on-Hudson
Courtesy of Westchester County Historical Society

Westchester was founded to provide funds for arts groups and promote the arts in Westchester. Corporations have led the fund raising efforts of the Council of the Arts. PepsiCo, Inc., in cooperation with the State University of New York at Purchase, created the outstanding Summerfare program which brings world-famous musical, theater, and dance groups to the S. U. N. Y. Purchase campus for a month of performances in July and August.

Well-known performing artists have always found Westchester an attractive place to live because of its proximity to New York and the privacy offered by its secluded countryside. Julius LaRosa, Colleen Dewhurst, Joan Bennett, Roberta Peters, Aaron Copeland, and Robert Merrill are among the celebrities who live in Westchester. They have given generously of their time and talents at many benefits which helped worthy organizations raise funds in Westchester.

The relocation to Westchester of several corporate headquarters during the decades after World War II had a major impact on the county. General Foods was the first, in 1953, followed by Ciba-Geigy, in 1956, and Nestle, in 1958.

In the 1960s and 1970s many factors combined to influence the corporate giants to move their vast operations to Westchester. They had the opportunity to build their own facilities, an available work force, and the interstate road system; Westchester County Airport made the county easily accessible to the rest of the northeast. Also, New York City had become less attractive as rents and taxes rose and the environment decayed.

Edwin G. Michaelian, county executive from 1956 to 1972, and William L. Butcher, chairman of the County Trust Company, were among those who were instrumental in selling Westchester County to the corporations. Lowell M. Schulman developed the corporate parks that grace both sides of the Cross Westchester Expressway. Among the companies along the "Platinum Mile" of interstate I-287 are A.M.F., Hitachi, Gannett Westchester Rockland Newspapers, Combe International, A.C.L.I., Texaco, and General Foods. Corporate parks were also developed on other major arteries. Robert Martin Company, founded by Martin S. Berger and Robert F. Weinberg, developed the Cross Westchester Executive Park in Elmsford in 1966 and the South Westchester Executive Park in Yonkers in the 1970s. They constructed many of the office buildings along Route 287 and in White Plains as well as houses and condominiums.

New Court House and urban renewal construction, White Plains
Photograph by Susan Swanson

The handsome architecture and landscaping of many of the corporate buildings make a significant contribution to the beauty of the county. In several instances, major architectural talents have been engaged to design buildings for such corporations as Union Carbide, Frank B. Hall, I.B.M. World Trade Americas/Far East, and PepsiCo. Their landscaped settings have provided Westchester with acres of parkland that complement the parks and parkways built in the 1920s.

In the past ten years, many business areas in Westchester communities have undergone extensive revitalization. White Plains, for instance, has undergone vast changes even since 1970. A new courthouse, a library, and many new department stores have been built. On the site of the old railroad station a new transportation center, office building, and world-class hotel are planned.

While there are many new buildings being built in Westchester today, there is a significant movement to retain fine old ones, and many landmarks have been renovated to be used as schools, colleges, and business offices. The Westchester Preservation League has worked with both individuals and municipalities to create historic districts and to save worthy buildings.

Private foundations have generously donated funds for historic preservation. None has done more than the Rockefeller family. Their creation of Sleepy Hollow Restorations, Incorporated, has preserved Van Cortlandt Manor, Philipsburgh Manor, and Sunnyside. Local efforts by non-profit historical societies and town historians continue to keep Westchester's heritage alive through historical museums, library collections, programs, and events.

Government agencies have also supported the historic preservation of Lyndhurst, Philipse Manor Hall in Yonkers, and the John Jay Homestead. In October 1981 the county of Westchester was bequeathed the beautiful estate, Merestead, in Mount Kisco, by Mrs. Margaret Sloane Patterson.

As Westchester County celebrates its 300th anniversary in 1983, residents can look with pride at the past 300 years and, with that rich heritage behind them, look with confidence to the next 300 years.■

Onatru Farm, Lewisboro

Farming continued to be an important occupation in northern Westchester in the 1920s. Onatru Farm, on Elmwood Road in Lewisboro, was a typical working farm. In fact, Edward Lane, who purchased it in 1905, named it Onatru because he wanted to live "on a true" farm. The farm was good-sized, 127 acres, and the family raised corn, hay, vegetables, fruit, dairy cattle, and small animals.

Alice Lane continued to work her parents' farm after her marriage to Walter Poor in 1915, and through her interest it continued to *prosper.*

Beginning in 1962, Onatru Farm was deeded to the town of Lewisboro in several stages. Town offices now occupy the second floor of the main house, and Northern Westchester Performing Arts and other non-profit groups use the first floor for their activities. A town park, a wildlife preserve, and a scouting reservation now occupy the surrounding fields and woods of Onatru. Photograph from History of Lewisboro

Ladies Aid Society of Methodist (United) Church, Armonk

The Ladies Aid Society of the Armonk Methodist (United) Church gathered here in the church lecture room in the late 1920s for mornings of companionship and quilting.

Many of the women were descendants of families that had lived in North Castle for over 200 years. Their great-grandmothers had probably also gathered together to quilt.

The ladies are (sitting, left to right): Sarah Findlay, Lucretia Remsen, Lilias Brundage, Lottie Hunter, Lillian Peck, Annie S. Acker, Sarah "Sadie" Johnson, Anna Blank, Ella L. Haviland, Martha Yerks, Mary E. See, and Edna B. MacDonald. Standing, left to right: Mrs. Foster Taylor (wife of the minister), Lulu MacDonald, an unidentified woman, and Elizabeth M. Brundage. Courtesy of North Castle Historical Society

Paving Manville Road, Pleasantville

Manville Road in Pleasantville wasn't paved until 1928, as this photograph shows. Fewer automobiles and less traffic made the need for paved roads less pressing than in the more densely settled areas of the county.

Note the Rome Theatre marquee on the left and Garfield Gardner's gas station and General Motors dealership on the right. Courtesy of John Crandall, Pleasantville Historian

Manville Road, Pleasantville

This photograph shows the same section of Manville Road in Pleasantville as it is today. The house on the far left in the 1928 photograph is still standing, as is the Rome Theatre and the building that housed Gardner's garage. Photograph by Gray Williams, Jr.

Sutton Farm, Chappaqua

Farming began to decline north of White Plains during the Depression when stricter sanitary laws, rising taxes, and falling profits made dairy farming less profitable. A few farms, such as the Sutton farm photographed here in 1982, still operate, selling fruit, vegetables, and nursery products. Most farmers, however, found there was more money to be made by selling their land than by farming it. Photograph by Gray Williams, Jr.

Yorktown Grange Fair

Many new houses rose on farm fields and pastures in the northern towns of Cortlandt, Yorktown, and Somers in the 1950s and 1960s. The new home owners loved the country flavor of the Yorktown Grange Fair, pictured here in 1953. The fair has been held every fall since 1923 and still continues to attract many visitors to see exhibits of livestock, vegetables, and handicrafts. Courtesy of Westchester County Historical Society

155

Elephant Laying a Wreath at the Statue of Old Bet, Somers

Nineteen fifty-three marked the 130th anniversary of the erection of the Elephant Hotel in Somers as well as the thirtieth anniversary of the Yorktown Grange Fair. In Honor of both occasions. Ranee, a baby elephant, was brought to Somers to lay a wreath at the foot of Old Bet's statue.

Old Bet was honored in similar fashion in 1922 when Old John, a veteran of the Ringling Brothers and Barnum and Bailey elephant herd, was marched to Somers from Madison Square Garden in New York City. Photograph by Derbyshire; courtesy of Somers Historical Society

Bronx River Parkway, Hartsdale

This view of the Bronx River Parkway, taken about 1938, shows the Fenimore Road Bridge at Hartsdale. Note the early exit sign, the rustic wooden guardrails and the narrow, steep entrance ramp. The parkway has undergone extensive reconstruction in the past ten years to accommodate increased high-speed traffic, but much of the charm and beauty of the original plan remain. Courtesy of New York State Bureau of Publicity

Goats on the Bronx River Parkway, Bronxville

Construction on the Bronx River Parkway, the first automobile parkway in the world, began in 1916. The parkway was built not so much to relieve traffic congestion, but to create an attractive scenic roadway, while at the same time rehabilitating the badly contaminated Bronx River. The parkway was the brainchild of William L. Ward, the Republican leader, who held no official office, but exerted enormous influence, particularly in the far-seeing

plans for the county's roads, parks, and recreational facilities. The Bronx River Parkway was only the first section of an impressive highway system that was to change the face of the county.

In this photograph, taken along the Bronxville section of the parkway about 1918, a truck collects some local goats that had wandered onto the roadway. Courtesy of Bronxville Public Library

Philipse Manor Development, North Tarrytown

It was the Bronx River Parkway that really opened up the county to the automobile. It attracted middle income families prospering during the boom period of the 1920s. Developers began to build communities for young lawyers, bankers, doctors, and executives who worked in New York City. Philipse Manor development was built between 1910 and 1932 in the cow pastures west of Broadway in North Tarrytown. In the beginning, large comfortable homes were set on good-sized lots connected by straight roads. Later, as the demand for housing grew, many of the lots were subdivided and smaller homes built between the larger ones. The tiny trees that can be seen along the roads are now over fifty feet tall, but some of the original cow-pasture cedars still survive. Courtesy of Westchester County Historical Society

Shado-Lawn Real Estate Office, Hastings-On-Hudson

This real estate office of the Homeland Company, which developed Shado-Lawn in Hastings-on-Hudson, did a booming business in the mid-1920s. Note the sign at the door which says "The Wise Ones Are Buying Now!" Courtesy of Hastings-on-Hudson Public Library

Scarsdale Shopping Area

Eastman House, Scarsdale

The Medieval Revival style of architecture, commonly known as Tudor, reached a peak of popularity in lower Westchester County following World War I. The Eastman residence on Mamaroneck Road in Scarsdale is a fine example of the Tudor combination of warmth and elegance which attracted many people to this area. Louis Bowman, an architect who lived in Bronxville, built many Tudor houses in that village, including his home on Elm Rock Road. Pelham, Larchmont, and Mount Vernon, among other towns, have many fine Tudor homes. Other residential styles popular between World War I and the Depression included Spanish Colonial Revival, Mission, and the perennial Georgian and Federal Revival. Courtesy of Scarsdale Public Library

The Medieval Revival style was carried over into the business areas of many lower Westchester towns as shown in this photograph taken of the Scarsdale shopping area in 1925.

Shops, apartment houses, and even gas stations took on the Tudor look that during the 1920s became synonymous with stylish suburban living. Courtesy of Scarsdale Public Library

157

Main Street, Dobbs Ferry

By the 1920s many of Westchester's towns had developed into the communities we recognize today. Streets were paved, telephone and electric lines strung, and stores opened for business. One modern-day problem which does not appear in this photograph of Main Street, Dobbs Ferry in the 1920s, is a shortage of parking. There isn't a parking meter in sight. *Courtesy of Westchester County Historical Society*

First Traffic Light in Hastings-on-Hudson

Parking may not have been difficult, but automobile traffic operating under meager rules and regulations created many traffic jams and accidents.

This photograph illustrates a solution to such problems devised by Hastings-on-Hudson. This white kiosk, located at Warburton Avenue and Main Street, served both as the first village traffic light and as police headquarters. The traffic light was known affectionately as the Village Lighthouse and was hand operated. Apparently requests for directions were few and simple and could be answered by the two arrows, "New York" and "Albany."

About 1920 the quaint lighthouse was removed and an overhead traffic signal installed. A similar police booth still stands on the corner of the Boston Post Road and Pelhamdale Avenue in Pelham Manor. Courtesy of Hastings-on-Hudson Public Library

The Toonerville Trolley's Last Run and the Bus that Replaced It, Pelham

Although the commuter railroads continued to prosper, the trolleys which had linked so many Westchester towns finally succumbed to the automobile and bus.

This photograph was taken July 31, 1937, the day the trolley made its last run. Pelham turned into Toonerville for a day. The trolley ran with the full complement of cartoon characters, including the Terrible Tempered Mr. Bang, Mickey (himself) McGuire, and Powerful Katrinka, as well as cartoonist Fontaine Fox, and eighty-six-year-old James Bailey, the original motorman, who is shown standing in front of the trolley. Ed Brown, who later became Pelham Town Historian, stands on the left side of the trolley. To the left the bus that replaced the Toonerville stands ready to go. Courtesy of Pelham Historical Society

Yonkers Ferry

Jack Schwartzstein saw the need for a ferry from Yonkers to New Jersey to accommodate commuters and excursionists. He joined with Frank Romer Pierson, the eleven-term mayor of Tarrytown, to found the Westchester Ferry Company in 1923. The Yonkers ferry ran between the John J. Walsh docks in Yonkers and Alpine, New Jersey, from 1923 until 1956. About 200,000 cars and over a million passengers a year took the five-minute ride across the Hudson River on boats such as the Paunpeck, the Walsh, and the Resolute. Fares were five cents for pedestrians, fifteen cents for bicyclists, and fifty cents for cars.

Many people still recall ferry rides in the moonlight, fabulous views of the Palisades, and the man who played accordian or guitar for nickels. John D. Rockefeller, Sr., loved the ferry and knew all the crew members by name.

Business dropped dramatically after the Tappan Zee Bridge opened in December 1955. In fact, the ferry went out of business within a year. Courtesy of Hudson River Museum, Yonkers

A Westchester Candidate for the World's Commuting Record: H. S. Chapman of Katonah, N. Y.

In the July 12, 1929, issue of the New York Telegram, Herbert S. Chapman of Katonah claimed the world's record for commuter travel, both for distance and for punctuality. Mr. Chapman, a supervisor in an insurance company in New York, had been catching the 6:40 to the city every day for thirty-nine years.

"I hope to keep on this way until I die," Chapman stated. "Regularity has been the secret of my life and I could not endure to disturb it. It leads to satisfaction and then to happiness.

"I always get up at 5:30, and my wife, bless her, in thirty-six years of married life never has let me go without breakfast or get my own breakfast. Then I saunter down to the station for the train. You couldn't keep up for thirty-nine years if you tried a mad, nervous dash for the train."

Mr. Herbert S. Chapman's record was 1,046,938 miles of commuting. In thirty-nine years he missed the train only twice. Courtesy of Mount Kisco Historical Committee

Commuters at Scarsdale Railroad Station

During the 1920s, commuters crowded into the Hudson, Putnam, Harlem, and New Haven trains in ever-increasing numbers. Any dyed-in-the-wool commuter will immediately recognize why the people awaiting the morning train at the Scarsdale railroad station are standing in three distinct groups. Their lives, like Mr.

Chapman's, are made more secure by regularity; they know where each car will stop and where they will board. Reading the paper is acceptable early-morning behavior; engaging in conversation is not. Courtesy of Scarsdale Public Library

Women Organize to Re-elect George C. Appell, Pleasantville

Men joined clubs for fun and fellowship as well as for raising funds to help worthy causes. In this 1923 photograph members of the Pelham Men's Club spoofed for the camera during their annual barbecue. The Pelham Men's Club is still active today and provides scholarships for Pelham High School students. Courtesy of Pelham Historical Society

The members of the Executive Committee of the Non-Partisan Committee for the Re-election of Judge George C. Appell as Judge of the Children's Court met in Pleasantville in 1928 to plan their campaign. They are, left to right: Mrs. Lyndon L. Lee, Mrs. William L. Archer, Mrs. Paul Borchard, Mrs. George C. Appell, Mrs. Julian C. Chase (chairman), Mrs. Frank A. Vanderlip, Mrs. C. Neal Barney, Mrs. Maurice Zuckert, Miss Judith Blanchard, and Mrs. Edgar Goldstein.

Women's organizations developed rapidly in Westchester in the 1920s. They provided an outlet for womens' interests and needs while providing many educational, cultural, political, and social services for their communities. This group was instrumental in Judge Appell's re-election. He resided in Mount Vernon and was also president of the New York Association of Children's Court Judges. Courtesy of John Crandall, Pleasantville Historian

Men's Club Barbecue, Pelham

Roller Coaster at Rye, Playland

The county of Westchester developed recreational parks throughout the county during the 1920s and 1930s. The roller coasters and amusement park at Playland in Rye became one of the greatest recreational attractions in the New York area.

The county bought 215 acres along the Rye shore in 1923, demolished the existing food stands and honky-tonk amusements, and integrated the beach and amusement park in an attractive setting with gardens and fountains. Playland was opened to the public in 1928 and continues to attract thousands to its park every summer. Courtesy of Westchester County Historical Society

AEROPLANE COASTER CURVES AT LIGHTNING SPEED — PLAYLAND, Westchester Co. Park System, RYE, N.Y.

Westchester County Center, White Plains

The Westchester County Center was part of the Westchester County Parks Commission's overall recreational plan for the county. It was designed in the fashionable art deco style by Walker and Gillette in 1930 as an all-purpose building for county functions.

The enormous flat floor of the County Center has accommodated everything from circuses to car shows; the building has a seating capacity of 4,200. Photograph from Sanchis, American Architecture: Westchester County

Armonk Airport

Another great recreational attraction in the 1920s and 1930s was Armonk Airport. Armonk "was the place people drove out to," according to North Castle Historian Richard Lander. Hundreds of automobiles crowded Old Bedford Road on their way to the airport. In the words of the North Castle Sun of October 10, 1924, "Last Sunday represented the largest crowd of visitors to this section seen this year.... The human herd is certain to increase as the years go by."

The crowds came to watch Clifford Payton's stunt flying, the barnstorming, and the parachutists, or to take a plane ride themselves for five dollars a head. Roadside stands and the Log Cabin Restaurant catered to their needs for food and drink. Residents still recall the phenomenal traffic jams along Bedford Road that took place on summer weekends.

Armonk Airport was located opposite MacDonald Avenue along Bedford (now Old Bedford) Road. A few of the original buildings still stand, but most, including the hangars, were razed to make room for the widening of Routes 22 and 684 in the 1970s. By that time, Westchester County Airport, begun in 1942 as a wartime airbase, had replaced Armonk Airport as the county's major airport. Courtesy of North Castle Historical Society

Charles Lindbergh

Charles Lindbergh created a sensation when he flew into Armonk Airport on August 5, 1928, to visit Mr. and Mrs. R. M. Lewis of Bedford Center. Although Lindy's arrival had been kept secret, word slipped out, and over 1,000 spectators cheered the hero as he landed his B-IX Brougham. Special detectives had to clear the way for him to reach the Lewis's car. A local newspaper reported that the next morning about 8:30 Lindbergh bade "good-bye to the crowd with the usual wave of his hand. He donned his helmet, climbed into the cockpit of the 'Love Eagle' and made a beautiful get-away." Courtesy of North Castle Historical Society

The *Hindenburg* Flies Over Yorktown

One of the world's great wonders in its time, the zeppelin, Hindenburg, *was photographed as it flew over Yorktown in 1936.*

The Hindenburg was 803 feet long and powered by four 1,100-horsepower Mercedes-Benz diesel engines. It cruised at seventy-eight miles per hour. The ship could carry up to fifty passengers within its hull. In 1936 the Hindenburg made ten trans-Atlantic crossings averaging about two-and-a-half days each between Germany and the United States.

On May 6, 1937, the Hindenburg burst into flames as it approached the airport at Lakehurst, New Jersey. Thirty-six people died in the tragic accident caused, it is believed, by atmospheric electricity igniting the hydrogen that filled and suspended the ship. *Courtesy of Westchester County Historical Society*

Amelia Earhart and Friends

Amelia Earhart Putnam is pictured here aboard her husband's yacht, together with the men who served as her assistants. The members of the group are (left to right): Harry Manning, navigator; Amelia Earhart; Fred Noonan, navigator; and Paul Mantz, technical advisor.

Miss Earhart, who resided in Harrison, became Westchester's own heroine when she was the first woman to make a solo flight across the Atlantic Ocean from Harbor Grace, Newfoundland, to Londonderry, Ireland, on May 20 and 21, 1932. On June 27, 1932, she was honored with a parade and a ceremony at the Harrison Town Park, where a bronze plaque featuring a propeller was unveiled.

That evening, in her honor, a militia band offered music at a dinner for over 500 guests at the Westchester Country Club.

Amelia Earhart disappeared during an attempt to fly over the Pacific Ocean in 1937. Fred Noonan, who is third from the left in the photograph, was also on the plane when it was lost. *Courtesy of Charles Dawson History Center, Harrison*

Perhaps the most glamorous industry in Westchester in the early 1920s was film-making. D. W. Griffith created a studio complex on Orienta Point, Mamaroneck, on the property of the railroad and hotel magnate Henry Flagler.

The talented Gish sisters, Lillian and Dorothy, photographed here in a scene shot at the studio, lived nearby on the corner of Bleeker and Walton avenues in a house designed in 1889 by Stanford White.

"In those days the area was less an 'East coast Hollywood' than Hollywood was a 'West coast Mamaroneck,' " recalled Joseph Rigano, a former studio employee, in a New York Times article of June 19, 1977. Courtesy of Westchester County Historical Society

A Burning Barn Becomes Part of a Film, Mamaroneck

Early film studios had none of the sophisticated sets and equipment taken for granted today. So, when the fire whistle blew in Mamaroneck, Griffith shouted at his cameramen and actors to follow him to the fire. Magaphone in hand, he startled firemen and spectators by instructing his actors to run in and out of the burning barn carrying people, papers, and animals. He then proceeded to write a script around the film footage.

A photograph of this episode is shown here. The man is carrying a girl in dark stockings. Courtesy of Westchester County Historical Society

Filming of America, Somers

The most ambitious film produced by D. W. Griffith while he was in Mamaroneck was the documentary *America*.

Griffith, the son of Civil War General Jacob Wark Griffith, wanted to create a film about the Revolution which would embody the ideals of liberty and democracy for which so many Americans had died in World War I. Prominent historians, members of patriotic societies, government officials, and members of the armed services all contributed to the production of the film. A special train took actors from Boston to Virginia to film important episodes of the Revolution at the historic sites where they had occurred. Hundreds of Revolutionary War descendants offered their services as extras in the film. Sinclair Weeks, secretary of war, loaned Griffith large numbers of soldiers for the battle scenes. General Wainwright personally led his Third Cavalry in the re-enactment of Morgan's Raid.

Somers was the scene of the filming of the Battle of Concord Bridge. Over 1,000 cars jammed the area as spectators came from all over Westchester to view the filming. The director noticed the need for a road just before the filming was to begin. " 'Blondy,' he yelled to his general superintendent, 'make a road.' And a road was made" (Mamaroneck Paragraph, October 25, 1923).

This photograph, taken at Somers, shows the patriot troops firing from behind stone walls along the hill. Note the extra lounging on the running board of his car as a friend repairs the right front tire. Courtesy of Somers Historical Society

Depression Relief Workers, Hastings-on-Hudson

Westchester suffered the miseries of the Depression along with the rest of the nation. But local work projects produced much that was worthwhile as well as providing employment to hundreds of Westchester residents.

Hastings-on-Hudson organized teams of relief workers to clean up unsightly vacant lots in the village. This group of men took a break beside their pile of collected debris and clowned for the photographer about 1935. Courtesy of Hastings-on-Hudson Historical Society

WPA Swimming Pool, Pleasantville

Residents of Pleasantville are shown in this picture watching swimming races at the village pool. It was constructed in 1934 by WPA workers using materials donated by local merchants. The pool, which is still enjoyed today, was built on Lake Street to replace the local swimming hole in Nanny Hagen Brook. Courtesy of John Crandall, Pleasantville Historian

CCC Workers at Ward Pound Ridge Reservation, Cross River

During the Depression a Civilian Conservation Corps camp was located at Ward Pound Ridge Reservation. Here workers posed for a photographer outside the snack bar they were constructing. The snack bar serves today as the Trailside Museum and Delaware Indian Resource Center on the reservation, which is operated by the Westchester County Department of Parks, Recreation and Conservation. Courtesy of Trailside Museum, Westchester County Department of Parks, Recreation and Conservation

DeWitt Wallace and Editor of the
***Reader's Digest*, Pleasantville**

DeWitt and Lila Acheson Wallace began the
Reader's Digest *in a basement below a Green-*
wich Village speakeasy in 1922. Within a few
months they moved to the suburban village of
Pleasantville, where they published the magazine
out of their home. As the Reader's Digest
grew, office space was rented in the village of
Pleasantville. Editorial offices were housed in
both the Mount Pleasant Bank building and the
County Trust building.

In this photograph (left to right) managing
editor Kenneth Payne meets with DeWitt Wal-
lace and Ralph Henderson, who later became
the first editor of the Digest's Condensed Books.
Courtesy of the Reader's Digest

***Reader's Digest* Mail Room, Pleasantville**

The Reader's Digest *quickly became a busi-*
ness large enough to employ over 300 Pleasant-
ville residents. About 10,000 pieces of mail
were opened and sorted by hand every day in this
mail room in 1936. Today Reader's Digest
receives between a half million and several
million pieces of mail per week, opened and
sorted by computer. Courtesy of the Reader's
Digest

Glen Island Casino, New Rochelle

Glen Island Casino, on the site of Starin's Glen
Island Resort of the 1890s, offered the public of
Westchester a welcome respite from the worries
of the Depression. These waiters stood ready to
serve the hundreds of diners who also came to
dance to the music of the big bands. Here, at the
Casino overlooking Long Island Sound, Glen
Miller, Tommy Dorsey, Benny Goodman, and
many others created the sound of "swing."
Courtesy of Westchester County Historical
Society

The *Pelham Sun* Donates its Handpress
to the Scrap Metal Drive, Pelham

Even before the United States entered World
War II, Westchester residents displayed their
pro-Allied sentiments by holding drives to
collect scrap metal for the British war effort. In
this picture members of the staff of the Pelham
Sun donated their old handpress. Other un-
usual pieces of scrap iron were donated in the
county. One of these, donated by Hastings-on-
Hudson resident Hamilton Cochran, was a
British cannonball, fired at the Battle of
Monmouth during the Revolutionary War. The
cannonball traveled in the captain's cabin on a
ship carrying the scrap back to Britain and was
received by a military honor guard in South-
ampton. Courtesy of Pelham Historical Society

Local Boys Enlist, Baldwin Place

Two young men from Baldwin Place in the town of Somers shake hands outside the post office after signing up for military duty in July 1942. Courtesy of Somers Historical Society

Pelham War Council First Aid Class

All over Westchester County, citizens took first-aid classes to learn how to care for casualties in case of an enemy attack. In this 1942 photograph, Pelham men practised bandaging one another in the high school gymnasium. Courtesy of Pelham Historical Society

Larchmont Acres Apartments (aerial view)

Following World War II, Westchester entered a period of prosperity and optimism somewhat similar to the 1920s. High-rise apartment complexes such as Larchmont Acres, shown in this aerial view, were an important part of the residential building boom of the 1950s. Strictly utilitarian brick apartment buildings were built after World War II as compared with the more romantic Tudor apartments of the 1920s. Courtesy of Westchester County Historical Society

Wild Oaks Village, Lewisboro

Wild Oaks Village was developed by George Ojarovsky, who purchased 330 acres in Lewisboro in the early 1960s. He wished to create a community where a young couple could start out in a moderately priced apartment, move up to a townhouse, and eventually purchase a single-family home without having to move out of the neighborhood. The plan called for a 50-unit garden apartment complex, 100 townhouses, and 29 single-family homes. By 1981 60 percent of Wild Oaks had been completed. Photograph from History of Lewisboro

Heritage Hills of Westchester, Somers

The Heritage Development Group created this condominium community in Somers to meet the needs of an increasing population of older people who prefer easy maintenance of their property. Henry J. Paparazzo, who had successfully developed Heritage Village in Southbury, Connecticut, began a similar community in Somers in 1973. Heritage Hills offers a choice of condominiums in a variety of groupings, set among the hills and valleys of the 1,000-acre site. Recreational facilities include a golf course, tennis courts, and a recreation hall with a swimming pool and saunas.

Ownership is restricted to residents over the age of forty with children over the age of eighteen. It is the largest planned adult community in Westchester. Courtesy of Heritage Development Group, Inc.

Washington's Headquarters Condominiums, Dobbs Ferry

Condominiums have been built in Westchester in large numbers since the 1970s. The Washington's Headquarters condominiums, erected in Dobbs Ferry on Broadway, have proved to be a popular alternative for young couples who cannot afford a single-family house as inflation raises mortage rates and real estate prices. They are also popular with older residents and with families without children. Courtesy of Greenburgh Public Library

Pelham Country Club

In this 1950s photograph children at the Pelham Country Club take off in a swimming race to the cheers of their parents.

Pelham Country Club, like many clubs in Westchester, was founded primarily as a golf club in the 1890s. The swimming pool was added in the late 1940s, when the club began to offer more services to the entire families of its members. Memberships in country clubs and shore clubs soared in the affluent 1950s and 1960s as more families were able to afford the good life in Westchester. Courtesy of Pelham Historical Society

Paddle Tennis, Scarsdale

Platform tennis or "paddle tennis" was invented by Fessenden S. Blanchard and James K. Cogswell, tennis enthusiasts who wished to play the game all year round. They built an all-weather court on Cogswell's property on Old Army Road just north of Ardsley Road. Playing equipment was adjusted to the new court. A large wooden paddle, similar to a ping-pong paddle, replaced the tennis racket, and a sponge rubber ball replaced the tennis ball. Paddle tennis had been born. Both Blanchard and Cogswell were members of the Fox Meadow Tennis Club, where the first platform for the new game was built in 1931. Platform tennis, which is played in the late fall, winter, and early spring, gained great popularity in Westchester after 1960. Every March the National Platform Tennis Men's Doubles Championship Tournament is played at the Fox Meadow Tennis Club. Courtesy of the Scarsdale Public Library

Children's Pet Show, Bronxville

The children's pet show at the Bronxville High School was a popular event during the 1950s. Here a proud young lady puts her pet through his paces for the judges. Youngsters at the Yorktown Grange Fair showed pigs, goats, and lambs, but in densely settled Bronxville, dogs, cats, and rabbits were favored. Courtesy of the Bronxville Public Library

Fresh Air Children, Scarsdale

Halloween Painting Contest, Scarsdale

Nine hundred and thirty Scarsdale youngsters competed in the Halloween window-painting contest pictured here in 1953. The contest was so popular that 250 six- and seven-year-olds had to be eliminated because of the shortage of available store windows. The Reporter Dispatch of November 2, 1953, reported that an estimated 6,500 people jammed the Scarsdale shopping area to view the windows over Halloween weekend. The grand award winner was fourteen-year-old Mary E. Klein.

The Halloween window-painting contest is just as popular today. Courtesy of Scarsdale Public Library

Many Westchester residents open their hearts and their homes to children from New York City during the summer months. In this photograph, Scarsdale families participating in the Fresh Air Program greet their city guests at the railroad station on a hot summer's day about 1955.

The Fresh Air Fund was originally the idea of millionaire D. Ogden Mills in the 1890s. Mills donated thousands of dollars to bring New York City children to the country he had loved as a boy. The Fresh Air Fund and other similar programs sponsored by local communities in Westchester are still very much in evidence. Courtesy of Scarsdale Public Library

Sarah Lawrence Students Picket Woolworth's, Bronxville

The good life in Westchester did not necessarily diminish social conscience, particularly among young people of the county. Many enthusiastically endorsed the Civil Rights movement of the early 1960s. Sarah Lawrence students picketed the Woolworth's building in Bronxville in the spring of 1960 to support the effort to integrate the company's lunch counters in the South. Courtesy of Bronxville Public Library

Junior League Volunteers, Scarsdale

Many young women in the county found satisfaction in working for service organizations such as the Junior League. They contributed thousands of volunteer hours on projects like the restoration of historic Wayside Cottage in Scarsdale. Husbands also offered their help on occasion as seen in this photograph. Note the young supervisor in the background, soda in hand, holding onto his mother's hand. Courtesy of Scarsdale Public Library

Wayside Cottage, Scarsdale

Picturesque Wayside Cottage, headquarters of the Scarsdale Junior League, is located on the White Plains Post Road (Route 22) and Wayside Lane in Scarsdale.

Built between 1715 and 1730, the cottage was owned by Michael Varian, a staunch patriot during the Revolution. Bullet holes through the shingles and saber slashes near the door are testimony to a British raid in October 1776. Following the Revolution, the Varians operated the cottage as a drovers' inn.

In 1853 Wayside Cottage was purchased by Charles Butler. It was later deeded to the town by his daughter, Emily Butler, in 1919 and was used for town meetings and as a library. After lying vacant for several years, the building was leased and restored by the Junior League. Courtesy of the Scarsdale Public Library

Caramoor Concert, Katonah

The quality of life in Westchester continues to be one of its major attractions. One of the many cultural attractions available to the public is the beautiful mansion, Caramoor, located off Route 22 in Katonah, which presents an outstanding series of music concerts every summer. These concerts are held in the Spanish courtyard or the Venetian theater on the estate, which was built by Walter and Lucie Rosen between 1930 and 1939 to house their unique collection of European and Chinese art.

The house-museum was opened to the public in 1970 after Mrs. Rosen's death. European furniture, paintings, sculpture, and tapestries dating from the Middle Ages are on display as well as complete rooms brought from European villas and palaces.

The house is open to the public for tours. Photograph by Victoria Beller Smith; courtesy of Caramoor Center for Music and the Arts, Inc.

Hudson River Museum, Yonkers

Another major cultural attraction in the county is the Hudson River Museum, located on Warburton Avenue in Yonkers. The museum complex includes art galleries, a planetarium, and a branch of the Yonkers Public Library, all built around Glenview, the mansion built by financier John Bond Trevor in 1876.

The city of Yonkers bought Glenview in 1924 and created the Yonkers Museum of Science and Arts. It broadened its scope and became known as the Hudson River Museum in 1939. A modern addition was added and Glenview restored to its original appearance in 1969. Courtesy of Hudson River Museum, Yonkers

Hammond Museum, North Salem

The Hammond Museum, located on Deveau Road off Route 124 in North Salem, is one of Westchester's most unique museums. It was created by artist and author Natalie Hays Hammond in 1957 as a museum of the humanities. Along with exhibition galleries, it features an exquisite Japanese stroll garden. This garden contains both native and Oriental plants and trees which are combined to form an environment which truly reflects Japanese ideals of harmony, grace, and unity with nature. Museum goers can also enjoy luncheon or dinner on the museum's secluded terrace. Courtesy of the Hammond Museum, North Salem

The atmosphere is relaxed and casual at this outdoor concert on the S.U.N.Y. campus at Purchase. Two flutists entertain the audience as part of Summerfare, a series of arts performances sponsored by PepsiCo. PepsiCo is in fact S.U.N.Y.'s neighbor. Its beautiful headquarters are located across the street from the campus, on Anderson Hill Road. Courtesy of PepsiCo Summerfare

Some of the well-known entertainers who have made Westchester County their home include Tallulah Bankhead, who lived in Bedford; the popular singer, Julius LaRosa, who lives in Irvington, actress Colleen Dewhurst, who makes her home in South Salem; movie star Joan Bennett, and Roberta Peters, opera star who live in Scarsdale. Courtesy of Julius LaRosa, Colleen Dewhurst, Joan Bennett, and Roberta Peters

Joan Bennett, Scarsdale

Julius LaRosa, Irvington

Colleen Dewhurst, South Salem

Roberta Peters, Scarsdale

Robert Merrill, New Rochelle

Robert Merrill, the well-known bass-baritone, has made this comment about living in West-chester County:

> *Because of the nature of my work, I have been privileged to travel to many places throughout the world. However, I don't think that any place equals Westchester County for beauty and heritage. The parks, the streams, the waterfronts, the lovely homes, the business and industrial developments and the wonderful com-bination of all religions and ethnic backgrounds make for a wonderful com-bination of tranquility and excitement at the same time.*

> *The fact that we can relax and be ourselves and enjoy our personal privacy is a quality that is difficult to match anywhere else. We also get a kick out of the historical fact that our home is situated on Thomas Paine's farmland. How's that for history and heritage? Need we add more other than we just love being residents of Westchester County. Courtesy of Robert Merrill*

Building the New England Thruway, Rye

The construction of the interstate road system in Westchester in the late 1950s and 1960s had a tremendous impact on local real estate values and the growth of business in the county. Many houses had to be razed or moved as the thruway inched northward, a repetition of the upheaval seen in northern Westchester when the reservoirs were constructed. This photograph was taken about 1958, when the thruway, Route 95, was being built near the railroad station and Purchase Street in Rye. Courtesy of Rye Historical Society

Tappan Zee Bridge, Tarrytown

The Tappan Zee Bridge provided a crucial link between Westchester County and the New York Thruway. Except for the center span, the bridge, which was completed in 1955, is a causeway resting on piles driven 300 feet into the bottom of the Hudson River. Photograph by L. F. Stockmeyer; courtesy of the Historical Society of the Tarrytowns

General Motors Assembly Division, North Tarrytown

General Motors took over the old Maxwell-Biscoe plant in 1918, when it bought Chevrolet. About 1928 landfill operations began, and several acres were added on which to enlarge the plant. Car bodies, manufactured next door at the Fisher Body Plant, were sent to G. M. for assembly.

Since the 1960s, the plant has provided employment for large numbers of Cuban refugees. Courtesy of the Historical Society of the Tarrytowns

Indian Point Nuclear Plant, Buchanan

In 1964 the Consolidated Edison Company opened its first nuclear energy plant on Indian Point in Buchanan. The site was formerly Charles Southard's brickyard, a park of the Hudson River Day Line, and Fleischmann Manufacturing Company, makers of whiskey and yeast. Courtesy of Consolidated Edison

Cross Westchester Expressway Before Development, Harrison and White Plains

Leonard H. Davidow bought property on the north side of Westchester Avenue in Harrison from the Whitelaw Reid estate in the early 1950s. On the south side of what is now Route 287 he purchased the undeveloped property between Havilands Lane and Bryant Avenue in White Plains. Davidow recognized the potential of Westchester Avenue for business development, but he bought more than he could afford. It was said that if he had five cents in his pocket he would use it to buy a dollar's worth of real estate. Moreover he refused to sell the land to anyone who did not meet his high standards. His property came to be known as the Valley of the Moon.

This aerial view shows Route 287 as it appeared in March 1965, looking northwest from the intersection with the Hutchinson River Parkway. In the foreground can be seen the Boy Scout headquarters. I.B.M. stands alone north of the expressway, at 1000 Westchester Avenue. Photograph by Joseph Cardillo; courtesy of Lowell M. Schulman

Cross Westchester Expressway After Development

In this photograph, taken in 1975 of the same area, the Boy Scout headquarters is located toward the lower right corner, and the Hutchinson River Parkway winds northward at the upper right. Route 684 dissects the view in the middle. The overpass seen in the upper left corner leads to Anderson Hill Road, which extends to the cross-shaped PepsiCo headquarters on the right and the campus of S.U.N.Y. at Purchase on the left. Westchester County Airport hangars and runways can be seen in the extreme upper left-hand corner. At the center between Route 684 and 287, the I.B.M. complex is now accompanied by the Cross Westchester Corporate Park. Courtesy of Lowell M. Schulman

White Plains Corporate Park

Lowell M. Schulman is the man who made Leonard Davidow's dream a reality. He started buying property in 1963 and over the next twenty years has developed White Plains Corporate Park, south of Route 287, and the Cross Westchester Corporate Park, north of the highway. This view of White Plains Office Park, taken in 1976, shows 1025 and 925 Westchester Avenue and the A.M.F. building.

Schulman's company built the corporate parks as communities "to provide all the amenities of a town...within the naturalistic setting of rocks and trees" (Reporter Dispatch, January 22, 1974). Landscape architect Kaneji Domoto of New Rochelle designed the eye-catching sculpture in both parks. Photograph by H. Bernstein, Associates, Inc.; courtesy of Lowell M. Schulman

New General Foods Corporate Headquarters, Rye

Shown here is the construction of General Foods' spectacular new headquarters at the eastern end of the Cross Westchester Expressway in Rye. The building was designed by architect Kevin Roche in an attractive park setting, which includes a man-made lake. Photograph by K. R. Duer, Jr.; courtesy of the General Foods Corporation

I.B.M. Corporate Headquarters, Armonk

Thomas J. Watson, Jr., when he was president of I.B.M. from 1952 to 1961, was instrumental in bringing several I.B.M. facilities to Westchester County. In 1957 I.B.M. moved its research activity to northern Westchester from Poughkeepsie and its data processing division to the East Post Road in White Plains. In 1961 the Thomas J. Watson Research Center was opened in Yorktown Heights, and in 1962 I.B.M. purchased the Standard Vacuum Company Building at 1000 Westchester Avenue in Harrison.

In 1964 the I.B.M. corporate headquarters, pictured here, was opened on the site of Wenga Farm, the estate of New York financier Cornelius Agnew, in Armonk. Today I.B.M. is the county's largest employer (14,000 workers), and I.B.M. offices occupy more than five million square feet in Westchester. When the newest I.B.M. building, adjacent to the Manhattanville campus, opens in mid-1983, 478,000 more square feet will have been added. Courtesy of I.B.M. Corporation

Union Carbide Corporation, Tarrytown

Union Carbide bought the former James Butler estate in Eastview between the Saw Mill River Parkway and Route 9A and developed a campus-style research center there in 1957. In 1966 a master plan was developed for a corporate research office complex on the property which was completed in 1970. The beauty of the Butler Estate has been maintained in the attractive park-like setting. The stone walls and avenue of maple trees along Old Saw Mill River Road have been retained, and cars now pass under the glass-enclosed walkway which connects the northern and southern sections of the Spine Building. Courtesy of Union Carbide Corporation

Frank B. Hall, Inc. Headquarters, Briarcliff Manor

Mount Kisco architect Richard Kaeyer designed the headquarters of Frank B. Hall, Incorporated. Approximately thirteen acres of its property on Pleasantville Road have been landscaped and planted to take advantage of the wooded hillside. Modern office buildings complement the remodeled Tudor house, originally built by the Rockefellers for their minister, Harry Emerson Fosdick. The building now serves as a guesthouse for visiting business associates. Courtesy of Frank B. Hall, Incorporated

Axe Castle, Tarrytown

Many of the estates built between 1880 and 1910 have been preserved and are being used as business offices and school administration buildings.

Axe Castle is a fine example of a private preservation effort. The forty-five room mansion, formerly known as Carollcliff, was built between 1900 and 1910 by General Howard Carroll. General Carroll was a newspaperman who also served as inspector-general of the New York State troops during the Spanish-American War.

In 1941 the castle was bought by Emerson W. Axe and his wife, the former Ruth Houghton. It is now the headquarters of the Axe Houghton Stock Fund. Courtesy of E. W. Axe and Company, Incorporated

Estherwood, Dobbs Ferry

Located on Clinton Avenue in Dobbs Ferry, Estherwood is a French style mansion built in 1894-95 by James Jennings McComb. Now preserved as a staff residence of the Masters School for Girls, Estherwood contains a sixty-five-foot-long entrance hall with a balcony and marble staircase. Another interesting feature is its octagonal library, which Mr. McComb built to accommodate his octagonal desk. Courtesy of the Westchester County Historical Society

Hartford House, Valhalla

In 1957 Westchester County purchased West-view Farms, the 370-acre estate of A & P magnate John A. Hartford, to provide space for Westchester Community College.

The Hartford house, built in 1932, now serves as the college administrative building. The house was placed on the National Register of Historic Places in 1979.
Photograph by Francis Falkenbury

Leland Castle, College of New Rochelle

The College of New Rochelle, the first women's Catholic college in New York State, has preserved Leland Castle as its administration building. Leland Castle, or Castle View as it was first known, was designed by architect William T. Beers for Simeon Leland, manager of the luxurious Metropolitan Hotel in New York. Leland Castle was completed in 1859 as a summer home and weekend retreat.

Mother Irene Gill bought Leland Castle and opened the Ursuline Seminary for Girls there in 1897. The school became the College of St. Angela in 1904 and has been known as the College of New Rochelle since 1910. Until 1973 the castle was used exclusively by the Ursuline sisters, who then transferred ownership to the college and built a new convent on Willow Drive. Today Leland Castle contains the office of the president as well as the Castle Gallery. Courtesy of College of New Rochelle

On July 4, 1943, John D. Rockefeller, Jr., and his wife drove from Pocantico Hills to the dedication of Philipse Castle (now Philipsburgh Manor) in this 1902 electric runabout. The Rockefellers had donated $300,000 to restore the manor house to its colonial appearance.

To show support for the gas-rationing program of the government, 100 residents of Pocantico Hills rode in three haywagons, and Mrs. Nelson Rockefeller drove a three-seater buckboard, drawn by two horses. Courtesy of Rockefeller Archive Center, Pocantico Hills

Barnraising at Philipsburgh Manor, North Tarrytown

In the fall of 1981 the barn at Philipsburgh Manor was destroyed by fire, killing many of the farm animals which had been specially backbred to the size of their colonial-period ancestors.

Sleepy Hollow Restorations purchased a genuine colonial Dutch barn in upstate New York and, using methods two centuries old, erected it on the site of the old one. Richard Babcock, a barn expert who learned his craft from his grandfather, is shown at the center supervising his sons Clayton and David.

The new barn was completed in the summer of 1982, and more animals were housed there. Farm animals were very much smaller in colonial days. Sheep were the size of today's beaver and hen's eggs so small that cake recipes of the period often called for a dozen or more. Courtesy of Sleepy Hollow Restorations

Irvington Town Hall Theatre, Irvington

Many important Westchester buildings have been restored through the efforts of local non-profit organizations. One of the most interesting is this theater, located in the town hall at Irvington. The town hall was constructed in 1900 on Main Street. The theater is located on the second floor and was modeled after Ford's Theatre in Washington, D.C.

The renovation of the theater was spearheaded by the Town Hall Theatre Group under the supervision of architect Robert Reilley. Funds were donated by the village, by the Junior League of Westchester-on-Hudson, and by many individuals. Photograph by Russell Minnerly, courtesy of Irvington Town Hall Theatre, Inc.

Flandreau Cottage, Mamaroneck

The Flandreau cottage, located at 110 Mount Pleasant Avenue in Mamaroneck, has served as the rectory of St. Thomas's Episcopal Church since 1965.

Known as Vue de L'Eau, the French Second-Empire-style house was built by John N. Flandreau, member of an old Huguenot family, in 1867. The house sits on its original site high above the Boston Post Road overlooking Mamaroneck Harbor. Photograph by Grace Huntley Pugh

Muscoot Park, Katonah

The Westchester County Department of Parks, Recreation and Conservation has taken over a number of landmark properties in the county and has used them to provide programs and events for the public.

In 1975 the county opened Muscoot Park on Route 100 in Katonah. The beautiful Georgian Colonial house was purchased by Ferdinand Hopkins in 1880 and operated as a gentleman's farm. Today the county has farm animals on display as well as herb and vegetable gardens. The farm is open for tours.

Muscoot is also the headquarters of the Museum and Laboratory for Archeology (MALFA), a non-profit group which operates archeological digs at several Indian and colonial sites around the county. Photograph by Gray Williams, Jr.

Merestead, Mount Kisco

Merestead, which means "farmlands," was bequeathed to Westchester County in October 1981 by Mrs. Margaret Sloane Patterson, whose father William Sloane of the W. & J. Sloane furniture company built the house in 1906.

The Sloanes, who had come out of the city to visit friends, fell in love with the area and built Merestead as a country retreat. The Sloane's only child, Margaret, was born and raised in the house.

The house contains an outstanding collection of books and art objects and will be preserved in its present state for the public. Courtesy of the Patent Trader

Peacock at Merestead, Mount Kisco

Antony, one of five peacocks who grace Merestead, symbolizes the quiet luxury of this mansion (although when Antony squawks he is far from quiet). Mrs. Patterson's generosity has ensured the preservation of her estate as a museum to provide the public with a view of the gracious lifestyle of a bygone era. Nature lovers will enjoy walking along trails planned for the gardens, woods, and fields. Photograph by Susan Swanson

Acker, Clinton S. *Around Peekskill Since 1882.* Brooklyn: T. Gaus' Sons, 1961.

Albertson, J. Donald, and Varian, Mrs. Clarence J. *Historic Van Cortlandtville.* Van Cortlandtville, N. Y.: Van Cortlandtville Historical Society, 1976.

Allison, Charles Elmer. *The History of Yonkers.* New York: Wilbur B. Ketchum, 1896.

Atkins, T. Astley. *Adriaen Van der Donck; an Address Delivered Before the Westchester County Historical Society. . . .* Yonkers, N. Y.: Statesman Print, 1888.

Atkins, T. Astley. *The Manor of Philipsburg: a Paper Read Before The New York Historical Society. . . .* Yonkers, N. Y.: Yonkers Historical and Library Association, 1894.

Auxford, Peyton C. "Westcheser's Own Game." *Westchester World* 2 (Fall/Winter 1970/71): 22-25.

Baird, Charles W. *Chronicles of a Border Town; History of Rye, Westchester County, N. Y., 1660-1870.* 1871. Reprinted Harrison, N. Y.: Harbor Hill Books, 1974.

Barr, Lockwood. *Ancient Town of Pelham, Westchester County, New York.* Richmond, Va.: Dietz Press, Inc., 1946.

Barrett, Robertson T. *The Town of Bedford; a Commemorative History.* Bedford, N. Y.: 1955.

Bedford Historical Society. *A Decade of Progress, 1964-1973.* Bedford, N. Y.: 1973.

Bedford Historical Society. *A Short Historical Tour of the Town of Bedford.* Bedford, N. Y.: 1971.

Benedict, Russell Reed. "They Had So Many Castles They Didn't Know What To Do." *Westchester Life* 7 (Sept. 1951): 16, 31.

Berger, Kathy. "From 'Ragtime' to Riches; a Homeowner's Story." *Westchester Illustrated* 5 (March 1981): 8.

Bisland, Anna Lawrence. "William Van Duzer Lawrence." *The Villager* 46 (May 1974): 8-9, 20, 24.

Bolton, Robert, Jr. *A History of the County of Westchester from Its First Settlement to the President Time.* New York: Alexander S. Gould, 1848.

Bradbury, Anna R. *History of the City of Hudson, New York, With Biographical Sketches of Henry Hudson and Robert Fulton.* Hudson, N. Y.: Record Printing and Publishing Co., 1908.

Briarcliff Manor/Scarborough Historical Society. *A Village Between Two Rivers.* Briarcliff Manor, N. Y.: 1977.

"The Bronx River Parkway—the County's Scenic Drive." *Westchester County Update*, Jan. 1976, p. 1.

Brown, Helen Warren. *Mamaroneck 1661-1961.* Mamaroneck, N. Y.: Tercentennial Committee, 1961.

Canning, Jeff, and Buxton, Wally. *History of the Tarrytowns, Westchester County, New York, From Ancient Times to the Present.* Harrison, N. Y.: Harbor Hill Books, 1975.

Chappaqua Historical Society. *The Early Quaker Hamlet of Old Chappaqua.* New Castle, N. Y.: 1973.

Chappaqua Historical Society. *The Chappaqua Life of Horace Greeley.*...New Castle, N. Y.: 1974.

Clarke, Gilmore D. "The Cross County Parkway." *Our Westchester 7* (June 1932): 14-15.

Cornell, Thomas C. *Adam and Anne Mott: Their Ancestors and Their Descendants.* Poughkeepsie, N. Y.: A. V. Haight, 1890.

Counihan, Martha, O.S.U. "CNR's Leland Castle." *Westchester Illustrated 5* (Feb. 1981): 74.

Crandell, Richard F. *This Is Westchester; a Study of Suburban Living.* New York: Sterling Publishing Company Inc., 1954.

Creamer, Robert. *1664-1964: the Story of a Town.* Eastchester, N.Y.: 1964.

Dalphin, Marcia. *Fifty Years of Rye, 1904-1954.* Rye, N. Y.: 1955.

Dawson, Charles. *Harrison's Early Days.* Harrison, N. Y.: Union Savings Bank, 1975.

Duncombe, Frances R. *Katonah; the History of a New York Village and Its People.* Katonah, N. Y.: Katonah Village Improvement Society, 1961.

"Fisher Body on the Hudson." *Westchester Life 7* (April 1951): 14-15.

Flood, Thomas, III. "Peekskill Military Academy." In *Peekskill: a Journey Into History, 1839-1965.* Peekskill, N. Y.: 1965.

Folsom, Merrill. *Great American Mansions and Their Stories.* New York: Hastings House, Publishers, 1963.

Frank, George A. "Ceiling's Unlimited at Westchester Airport." *Westchester Life 9* (Feb. 1953): 17, 24.

Frank, George A. "Exodus...to Westchester." *Westchester Life 2* (Dec. 1952): 13-14, 35.

Franko, Alfred M. *The Place of Mount Vernon's Village Green and St. Paul's Church in American History.* Mt. Vernon, N. Y.: n.d.

French, Alvah P. *History of Westchester County, New York.* New York: Lewis Historical Publishing Company, 1925.

French, Alvah P. *Scrapbooks.* In Westchester County Historical Society Library.

Fulcher, William Gershom. *The Story of a Friendly Village: Mamaroneck, New York, 1896-1946.* Mamaroneck, N. Y.: Historical Committee of the Golden Jubilee Committee, 1946.

Griffin, Ernest Freeland, ed. *Westchester County and Its People: a Record.* New York: Lewis Historical Publishing Company, 1946.

Hamilton, Milton W. *Henry Hudson and the Dutch in New York.* Albany, N. Y.: State Education Department, 1964.

Hansen, Harry. *Scarsdale, From Colonial Manor to Modern Community.* New York: Harper and Brothers, 1954.

Harris, Jay. *God's Country; a History of Pound Ridge, New York.* Chester, Conn.: Pequot Press, 1971.

Hastings Centennial Chronicle. Hastings-on-Hudson, N. Y.: Hastings Historical Society, 1979.

A History of the Town of Lewisboro, Westchester County, New York. South Salem, N. Y.: Lewisboro History Book Committee, 1981.

Hodgson. Valentine M. "Old Stage Coach Days Recalled." *Westchester County Magazine* 9 (Sept. 1912): 81-82.

Hoffman, Renoda. *The Battle of White Plains*. White Plains, N. Y.: Battle of White Plains Monument Committee, 1976.

Hoffman, Renoda. *Yesterday in White Plains; a Picture History of a Vanished Era*. White Plains, N. Y.: 1981.

Holbrook, Stewart H. *The Old Post Road*. New York: McGraw Hill, 1962.

Horton, William Tompkins. *Pioneers, Patriots, and People: A History of Peekskill, N. Y.* Peekskill, N. Y.: Enterprise Press, 1953.

Howell, Ella. *Mamaroneck Scrapbook*, edited by Harold Dean Cater. In Westchester County Historical Society Library.

Huelle, Walter E. "Cyclone...in Westchester." *Westchester Life* 8 (Aug. 1952): 12-13, 25.

Huelle, Walter E. "The Great White Day After Christmas." *Westchester Life* 2 (Dec. 1952): 10-11, 27.

Hufeland, Otto. *Scrapbooks*. In Huguenot-Thomas Paine Historical Association Library.

Hufeland, Otto. *Westchester County During the American Revolution, 1775-1783*. White Plains, N. Y.: Westchester County Historical Society, 1926.

Hutchinson, Lucille and Theodore. *The Centennial History of North Tarrytown*. North Tarrytown, N. Y.: 1974.

Hutchinson, Lucille and Theodore. *Storm's Bridge: the History of Elmsford 1700-1976*. Elmsford, N. Y.: Bicentennial Committee of Elmsford, 1980.

"An Interview with Ruth Nichols." *Our Westchester*, Feb. 1921, p. 17, 36-37.

Lederer, Richard M., Jr. *The Place-Names of Westchester County, New York*. Harrison, N. Y.: Harbor Hill Books, 1978.

Lee, Frances Cook. *New Castle Historical Records...with a Pictorial History of the Town*. Chappaqua, N. Y.: 1977.

Lewis, Alvina Rich. "One Hundred Years; the Story of the Croton Aqueduct." Ossining Historical Society's *Museum Intelligencer*, May 5, 1943, p. 1, 6.

Life of a River Village: Dobbs Ferry. Dobbs Ferry, N. Y.: 1974.

Lindsley, Charles E. "The Huguenot Settlement of New Rochelle." *New Rochelle Pioneer*, Sept 5, 1885.

McDonald, John M. *McDonald Papers* (Photocopy of Unpublished Manuscript, 1844-1851). In Westchester County Historical Society Library.

Mathery, Alice Barber. "The Unpredictable Tallulah of Bedford Village." *Westchester Life* 7 (April 1951): 13, 31.

Mathias, A. H. "Hastings-on-Hudson." *Of Westchester* 4 (May-June 1972): 45-48.

Mays, Victor. *Pathways to a Village*. Bronxville, N. Y.: Nebko Press, 1961.

Miller, Louise Stevens. *Story of the Stevens House, 1851-1882*. Mount Vernon, N. Y.: Mount Vernon Public Library, 1951.

Mottelay, Paul F., and Campbell-Copeland, T., eds. *The Soldier In Our Civil War: a Pictorial History of the Conflict, 1861-1865*. New York: Stanley Bradley Publishing Company, 1890.

Nichols, Herbert B. *Historic New Rochelle*. New Rochelle, N. Y.:

Board of Education, 1938.

North Castle Historical Society. *North Castle History.* Various dates.

North Salem: a Pictorial Essay. North Salem, N. Y.: North Salem Free Library, 1979.

North Salem Historical Society. *Bulletin.* Various dates.

Northshield, Jane, ed. *History of Croton-on-Hudson, New York.* Croton-on-Hudson, N. Y.: Croton-on-Hudson Historical Society and Croton-on-Hudson Bicentennial Committee, 1976.

Oechsner, Carl. *Ossining, New York; an Informal Bicentennial History.* Croton-on-Hudson, N. Y.: North River Press, Inc., 1975.

"One Hundred Years of Railroads Here." Ossining Historical Society's *Intelligencer,* May 1949, p. 1, 5.

Owens, William A. *Pocantico Hills, 1609-1959.* Tarrytown, N. Y.: Sleepy Hollow Restorations, 1960.

Parrell, Sr. Mary Agnes. *Profiles of Dobbs Ferry.* Dobbs Ferry, N. Y.: Oceana Publications, Inc., 1976.

Portrait of a Village: Wolfert's Roost, Irvington-on-Hudson. Irvington, N. Y.: Washington Irving Press, 1971.

Potter, Virginia. "Inheriting a Chateau." *Westchester Life* 8 (Jan. 1952), p. 13, 21, 28.

Ray, Reginald P. "Historical Westchester." *Our Westchester,* March 1932, p. 26-27.

"A Relic of the Gay Nineties." Westchester County Realty Board's *Westchester,* Aug. 1935, p. 6.

Reynolds, Dunbar S. "Glen Island, World Wonder of the Elegant Eighties." *Westchester World,* 1974, p. 28-33.

Ritchie, William A. *Indian History of New York State; Part III—The Algonkian Tribes.* Albany, N. Y.: New York State Museum and Science Service, 1974.

Rosch, John. *Historic White Plains.* 1937. Reprinted Harrison, N. Y.: Harbor Hill Books, 1976.

Sanchis, Frank E. *American Architecture: Westchester County, New York, Colonial to Contemporary.* Croton-on-Hudson, N. Y.: North River Press, Inc., 1977.

Scharf, J. Thomas. *History of Westchester County, New York, Including Morrisania, Kings Bridge, and West Farms, Which Have Been Annexed to New York City.* Philadelphia: L. E. Preston and Co., 1886.

Seabury, Samuel. *Letters of a Westchester Farmer,* edited by Clarence H. Vance. White Plains, N. Y.: Westchester County Historical Society, 1930.

Seacord, Morgan H., and Hadaway, William S. *Historical Landmarks of New Rochelle.* New Rochelle, N. Y.: Huguenot Historical Association, 1938.

Shonnard, Frederick, and Spooner, W. W. *History of Westchester County.* 1900. Reprinted Harrison, N. Y.: Harbor Hill Books, 1974.

Silliman, Arthur W. *A Short Informal History of Ardsley, N. Y.* Ardsley, N. Y.: 1968.

Smith, Henry T. *Peekskill: A Friendly Town.* Peekskill, N. Y.: Friendly Town Association, 1952.

Snyden, Clifford L. *Somers Remembered.* Somers, N. Y.: Somers Historical Society, 1976.

Somers Historical Society. *The Elephant Hotel.* Somers, N. Y.: 1962.

Squire, Amos O. "History of Sing Sing Prison." Ossining Historical Society's *Intelligencer,* 1949, p. 3, 6.

Steinberg, Jay M. "Washington Irving and the 'Iron Horse.'" *Westchester Life* 7 (May 1951): 14, 34.

"Suffrage and Suffragists in Westchester." *Westchester Life of Today* 1 (Oct. 1915): 6-7, 11.

Swanson, Susan Cochran. *Between the Lines: Stories of Westchester County, New York, During the American Revolution.* Pelham, N. Y.. Junior League of Pelham, Inc., 1975.

Tatum, Edward H. *The Story of Larchmont Manor Park.* Larchmont, N. Y.: 1946.

"Through the Years—History of the New York & Harlem Railroad." *Club Dial* 34 (Nov. 1950): 21, 47-49.

Torres, Louis. *Tuckahoe Marble.* Harrison, N. Y.: Harbor Hill Books, 1976.

Van der Donck, Adriaen. *A Description of the New Netherlands.* Syracuse, N. Y.: Syracuse University Press, 1968.

"Viewing the Countryside." *Westchester Life of Today* 1 (Oct. 1915): 3.

Waldron, William Watson. *Huguenots of Westchester and Parish of Fordham.* New York: W. H. Kelly & Brother, 1864.

Walton, Frank L. *Pillars of Yonkers.* New York: Stratford House, 1951.

Warner, Fred C. "Tales of a Wayside Inn." *Westchester Life* 13 (June 1957): 10-11, 13.

Warner, Fred C. "What's In a Name?" *Westchester Life* 3 (Jan. 1953): 10-11, 23.

Weigold, Marilyn E. *America's Mediterranean.* Port Washington, N. Y.: Kennikat Press, 1974.

Weigold, Marilyn E. "Peekskill." *Westchester* 8 (Sept. 1976): 77-82, 105.

Weigold, Marilyn E. "Port Chester." *Westchester* 8 (Oct. 1976): 95.

Westchester County Historical Society. Library Clipping Files.

Westchester County Historical Society. *Quarterly Bulletin* and *Westchester Historian.* Various dates.

Yonkers Historical Society. *Bulletin.* Various dates.

Yonkers Through Three Centuries. Yonkers, N. Y.: Central National Bank of Yonkers, 1946.

Index

HISTORIC SITES AND MUSEUMS OF WESTCHESTER COUNTY, N. Y.

WESTCHESTER COUNTY HISTORICAL SOCIETY
75 Grasslands Rd., Valhalla; at Westchester Community College
Office: (914) 592-4323   Library: (914) 592-4338

BEDFORD 1829 SCHOOL HOUSE AND 1787 COURT HOUSE & MUSEUM
Beford Historical Society; Village Green, Bedford, NY
(914) 234-9367

BUSH HOMESTEAD; PORT CHESTER
Port Chester Historical Society; Lyon Park; 479 King St., Port
Chester, NY (914) 939-5830

ELEPHANT HOTEL; SOMERS
Somers Historical Society; Somers Town House; Routes 100 and 202;
Somers, NY (914) 277-3674

HAMMOND HOUSE; VALHALLA
Westchester County Historical Society; Route 100C, Grasslands Rd.,
Valhalla (Eastview), NY (914) 592-3175

JOHN JAY HOMESTEAD; KATONAH
A New York State Historic Site; Route 22, Jay St., Katonah, NY
(914) 232-5651

LYNDHURST; TARRYTOWN
A property of the National Trust for Historic Preservation;
635 South Broadway, Route 9, Tarrytown, NY (914) 631-0046

MARBLE SCHOOL HOUSE; EASTCHESTER
Eastchester Historical Society; California Rd., Eastchester, NY
(914) 793-1900

OSSINING HISTORICAL MUSEUM; OSSINING
Ossining Historical Society, 196 Croton Ave., Ossining, NY
(914) 762-4851

PHILIPSE MANOR UPPER MILLS; TARRYTOWN
A Sleepy Hollow Restoration; Route 9, North Tarrytown, NY
(914) 631-8200

PHILIPSE MANOR HALL; YONKERS
A New York State Historic Site; 29 Warburton Ave., Yonkers, NY
(914) 965-4027

QUAKER MEETING HOUSE, SCARSDALE
Scarsdale Historical Society; 937 Post Rd., Scarsdale, NY
(914) 723-1744

SHERWOOD HOUSE; YONKERS
Yonkers Historical Society; 340 Tuckahoe Rd., Yonkers, NY
(914) 965-1243

SMITH'S TAVERN; ARMONK
North Castle Historical Society; 440 Bedford Rd., Armonk, NY
(914) 273-3312

SQUARE HOUSE; RYE
Rye Historical Society; 1 Purchase St., Rye; (914) 967-7588

SUNNYSIDE; TARRYTOWN
A Sleepy Hollow Restoration; Route 9; South Broadway,
Tarrytown, NY (914) 631-8200

TARRYTOWN HISTORICAL MUSEUM; TARRYTOWN
Historical Society of the Tarrytowns; 1 Grove St., Tarrytown, NY
(914) 631-8374

THOMAS PAINE COTTAGE; NEW ROCHELLE
Huguenot & Thomas Paine Historical Association; 983 North Ave.
New Rochelle, NY (914) 632-5376

VAN CORTLANDT MANOR; CROTON-ON-HUDSON
A Sleepy Hollow Restoration; Route 9; Croton-on-Hudson, NY
(914) 631-8200

WASHINGTON'S HEADQUARTERS: NORTH WHITE PLAINS
Daughters of the American Revolution; Virginia Rd.,
North White Plains, NY (914) 949-1236

YORKTOWN MUSEUM; YORKTOWN HEIGHTS
Town of Yorktown; 1974 Commerce St., Yorktown Heights, NY
(914) 962-2970

Hours of sites and museums vary greatly.
Call for information